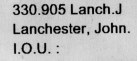
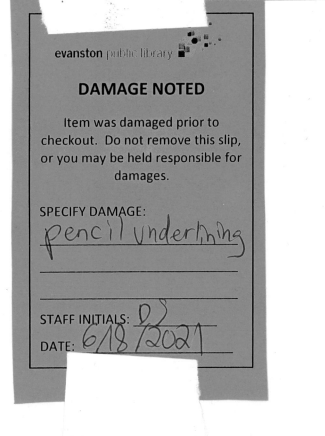

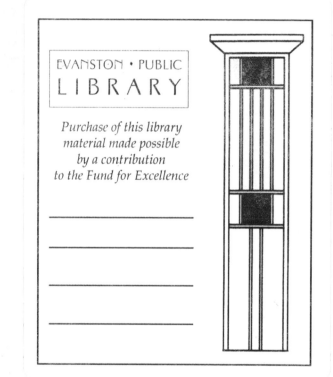

ALSO BY JOHN LANCHESTER

Family Romance

Fragrant Harbour

Mr. Phillips

The Debt to Pleasure

JOHN LANCHESTER

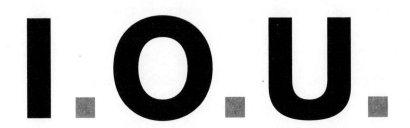

Why Everyone Owes Everyone and No One Can Pay

SIMON & SCHUSTER

New York London Toronto Sydney

Simon & Schuster
1230 Avenue of the Americas
New York, NY 10020

First Simon & Schuster hardcover edition January 2010

SIMON & SCHUSTER and colophon are registered trademarks
of Simon & Schuster, Inc.

For information about special discounts for bulk purchases,
please contact Simon & Schuster Special Sales at
1-866-506-1949 or business@simonandschuster.com

The Simon & Schuster Speakers Bureau can bring authors to
your live event. For more information or to book an event contact
the Simon & Schuster Speakers Bureau at 1-866-248-3049
or visit our website at www.simonspeakers.com.

Designed by Jaime Putorti

Manufactured in the United States of America

10   9   8   7   6   5   4   3   2   1

Library of Congress Cataloging-in-Publication Data

Lanchester, John.
I.O.U. : why everyone owes everyone and no one can pay /
John Lanchester.
      p.   cm.
Includes bibliographical references and index.
1. Global financial crisis, 2008–2009.   2. Economic history—21st
century.   3. International finance.   I. Title.
HB3722.L35   2010
330.9'0511—dc22   2009036465

ISBN 978-1-4391-6984-1
ISBN 978-1-4391-6987-2 (ebook)

For Miranda and Finn and Jesse

"When the capital development of a country becomes the by-product of a casino, the job is likely to be ill-done."
—*John Maynard Keynes,*
The General Theory of Employment,
Interest, and Money

"It's such a fine line between stupid and clever."
—*David St. Hubbins,* This Is Spinal Tap

CONTENTS

INTRODUCTION

Annie Hall is a film with many great moments, and for me the best of them is the movie's single scene with Annie's younger brother, Duane Hall, played by Christopher Walken, the first of his long, brilliant career of cinema weirdos. Visiting the Hall family home, Alvy Singer—that's Woody Allen—bumps into Duane, who immediately shares a fantasy:

"Sometimes when I'm driving . . . on the road at night . . . I see two headlights coming toward me. Fast. I have this sudden impulse to turn the wheel quickly, head-on into the oncoming car. I can anticipate the explosion. The sound of shattering glass. The . . . flames rising out of the flowing gasoline."

It's Alvy's reply which makes the scene: "Right. Well, I have to—I have to go now, Duane, because I, I'm due back on the planet Earth."

I've never shared Duane Hall's wish to turn across the road into the oncoming headlights. I have to admit, though,

that I have sometimes had a not-too-distant thought. It's a
thought which never hits me in town, or in traffic, or when
there's anyone else in the car, but when I'm on my own in
the country, zooming down an empty road, with the radio
on, and everything is moving free and clear, as it hardly
ever is with today's traffic, but when it is, I sometimes have
a fleeting thought, one I've never acted on and hope I never
will. The thought is this: what would happen if I chose this
moment to put the car into reverse?

When you ask car buffs that, the first thing they do is to
give you a funny look. Then they give you another funny
look. Then they explain that what would happen is that
the car's engine would basically explode: bits of it would
burst through other bits, rods would fly through the air,
the carburetor would burst into fragments, there would
be incredible noise and smell and smoke, and you would
swerve off the road and crash with the certainty of serious injury and the high probability of death. These explanations are sufficiently convincing that I find that the
thought of putting the car into reverse flits across my mind
only very temporarily, for about half a second at a time,
say once every two or three years. I'm sure it's something
I'll never do.

For the first years of the new millennium, the whole
planet was zooming along, doing the equivalent of seventy
on a clear road on a sunny day. Between 2000 and 2006,
public discourse in the Western world was dominated by
the election of George W. Bush, the attacks of 9/11, the
"global war on terror" and the wars in Afghanistan and
Iraq. But while all that was happening, something momen-
tous was taking place, not quite unnoticed but with bi-
zarrely little notice: the world's wealth was almost doubling.
In 2000, the total GDP of Earth—the sum total of all the

economic activity on the planet—was $36 trillion.* By the end of 2006, it was $70 trillion. In the developed world, so much attention was given to the bust in dot-com shares in 2000—"the greatest destruction of capital in the history of the world," as it was called at the time—that no one noticed the way the Western economies bounced back. The stock market was relatively stagnant, for reasons I'll go into later, but other sectors of the economy were booming. So was the rest of the planet. An editorial in *The Economist* in 1999 pointed out that the price of oil was now down to $10 a barrel, and issued a solemn warning: it might not stay there: there were reasons for thinking the price of oil might go to $5 a barrel. Ha!

By July 2008 the price of oil had risen to $147.70 a barrel, and as a result the oil-producing countries were awash with cash. From the Arab world to Russia to Venezuela, the treasury departments of all oil-producing countries resembled the scene in *The Simpsons* in which Monty Burns and his assistant, Smithers, pick up wads of cash and throw them at each other while shouting "Money fight!" The demand for oil was so avid because large sections of the developing world, especially India and China, were undergoing unprecedented levels of economic growth. Both countries suddenly had a hugely expanding, highly consuming new middle class. China's GDP was averaging growth of 10.8 percent a year, India's 8.9 percent. In fifteen years, India's middle class, using a broad definition of the term meaning the section of the population who had escaped from poverty, grew from 147 million to 264 million;

---

* GDP, which will be mentioned quite a few times in this story, sounds complicated but isn't: it's nothing more than the value of all the goods and services produced in an economy. GDP per capita, measuring each individual's piece of the country's pie, is the standard measure of prosperity.

China's went from 174 million to 806 million, arguably the greatest economic achievement anywhere on Earth, ever. Chinese personal income grew by 6.6 percent a year from 1978 to 2004, four times as fast as the world average. Thirty million Chinese children are taking piano lessons. Two-fifths of all Indian secondary school boys have regular after-school tuition. When you have two and a quarter billion people living in countries whose economies are booming in that way, you are living on a planet with a whole new economic outlook. Hundreds of millions of people are measurably richer and have new expectations to match. So oil is up, manufacturing is up, the price of commodities— the stuff which goes to make stuff—is up, the economy of (almost) the entire planet is booming. Who knows, optimists think, with the global economy growing at this rate, we can perhaps begin to think seriously about meeting the United Nations' Millennium Development goals, such as halving the number of hungry people, and of people whose income is less than $1 a day, by 2015.[1] That seemed utopian at the time the goals were set, but with the world $34 trillion richer, it suddenly looked as if this unprecedented target might be achieved.

And then it was as if the global economy went out one day and decided it was zooming along so well, there'd never be a better moment to try that thing of putting the car into reverse. The result . . . well, out of what seemed to most people a clear blue sky, the clearest blue sky ever, there was a colossal wreck. That left an awful lot of people wondering one simple thing: what happened?

I've been following the economic crisis for more than two years now. I began working on the subject as part of the background to a novel, and soon realized that I had stumbled across the most interesting story I've ever found.

While I was beginning to work on it, the British bank Northern Rock blew up, and it became clear that, as I wrote at the time, "If our laws are not extended to control the new kinds of super-powerful, super-complex, and potentially super-risky investment vehicles, they will one day cause a financial disaster of global-systemic proportions." I also wrote, apropos the obvious bubble in property prices, that "you would be forgiven for thinking that some sort of crash is imminent." I was both right and too late, because all the groundwork for the crisis had already been done—though the sluggishness of the world's governments, in not preparing for the great unraveling of autumn 2008, was then and still is stupefying. But this is the first reason why I wrote this book: because what's happened is extraordinarily interesting. It is an absolutely amazing story, full of human interest and drama, one whose byways of mathematics, economics, and psychology are both central to the story of the last decades and mysteriously unknown to the general public. We have heard a lot about "the two cultures" of science and the arts—we heard a particularly large amount about it in 2009, because it was the fiftieth anniversary of the speech during which C. P. Snow first used the phrase. But I'm not sure the idea of a huge gap between science and the arts is as true as it was half a century ago—it's certainly true, for instance, that a general reader who wants to pick up an education in the fundamentals of science will find it easier than ever before. It seems to me that there is a much bigger gap between the world of finance and that of the general public and that there is a need to narrow that gap, if the financial industry is not to be a kind of priesthood, administering to its own mysteries and feared and resented by the rest of us. Many bright, literate people have no idea about all sorts of economic basics, of a type that financial insiders take as elementary facts of how the world works. I am an outsider to finance and economics, and my hope is that I can talk across that gulf.

My need to understand is the same as yours, whoever you are. That's one of the strangest ironies of this story: after decades in which the ideology of the Western world was personally and economically individualistic, we've suddenly been hit by a crisis which shows in the starkest terms that whether we like it or not—and there are large parts of it that you would have to be crazy to like—we're all in this together. The aftermath of the crisis is going to dominate the economics and politics of our societies for at least a decade to come and perhaps longer. It's important that we try to understand it and begin to think about what's next.

ONE

THE ATM MOMENT

As a child, I was frightened of ATMs. Specifically, I was frightened of the first ATM I ever saw, the one outside the imposing headquarters of the Hongkong and Shanghai Bank, at 1 Queen's Road Central, Hong Kong. This would have been around 1970, when I was eight. My father, being an employee of the bank, was an early adopter of the ATM, which stood just to one side of the building's iconic bronze lions, but every time I saw him use it I panicked. What if the machine got its sums wrong and took all our money? What if the machine took someone else's money by mistake, and my father went to prison? What if the machine said it was giving him only ten Hong Kong dollars but actually took much more out of his account—some unimaginably large sum, like fifty or a hundred dollars? The freedom with which the machine coughed up its cash, and the invitation to go straight out and spend it, seemed horribly reckless. The flow of money, from our account out through the machine and then into the world, just seemed too easy. My dad would stand there grimly tapping in his PIN while I hung on to his arm and begged him to stop.

My scaredy-cat eight-year-old self was on to something. The sheer frictionlessness with which money moves around the world is frightening; it can induce a kind of vertigo. This can happen when you are reading the financial news and suddenly feel that you have no grip on what the numbers actually mean—what those millions and billions and trillions actually represent, how to get hold of them in your mind. (Try the following thought experiment, suggested by the mathematician John Allen Paulos in his book *Innumeracy*.[1] Without doing the calculation, guess how long a million seconds is. Now try to guess the same for a billion seconds. Ready? A million seconds is less than twelve days; a billion is almost thirty-two years.) Or it can happen when you look at a bank statement and contemplate the terrible potency of those strings of digits, their ability to dictate everything from what you eat to where you live—the abstract numerals whose consequences are the least abstract thing in the world. Or it can happen when the global flow of capital suddenly hits you personally—when your apparently thriving employer goes out of business owing to a problem with credit or your mortgage loan jumps unpayably upward—and you think: just what is this money stuff, anyway? I can see its effects—I can thumb a banknote, flip a coin—but what is it, actually? What do these abstract numbers stand for? What is the thing that's being represented? Wouldn't it be reassuring if it were more like a physical thing and less like an idea? And then the thought fades: money is what it always was, just there, a fundamental fact of the world, something whose coming and going are predictable in the way that waves are predictable on a beach: sometimes the tide is in, sometimes the tide is out, but at least you know the basic patterns of its movement operate under known rules.

And then something happens to change your sense of how the world works. For Rakel Stefánsdóttir, a young Icelandic woman studying for a master's degree in arts and cultural management at the University of Sussex in Brighton, it happened in early October 2008. She stuck her card into the wall to take out some cash, and the machine told her that the funds weren't available. Rakel thought nothing of it. "I know it goes through the transatlantic telephone line and that sometimes has problems, so I thought it must be that." A day or so earlier she had paid her first term's school fees on her card; she had been working in the theater for a number of years before going back to do this M.A. degree, and she was comfortably solvent.

We've all had the experience of sticking our card in the wall and not getting any money out of the ATM machine because we don't have any money in our account. But what Rakel, and thousands of other Icelanders that day, were experiencing was something much stranger and more unsettling. Her ATM card was blanking on her not because she didn't have the money but because the bank didn't. In fact, it wasn't just that the bank didn't have enough money, it was the *Apocalypse Now* scenario: her card wasn't working because Iceland had run out of money. On October 6 the government closed the banks and froze the movement of any capital outside the country because it was on the verge of going broke. By the time Rakel's credit card payment for her term's fees cleared, one day later, the Icelandic króna had collapsed and the amount she shelled out had increased by 40 percent. It took three weeks for Rakel to regain access to her bank account, and by that time it had become clear that her course of studies was unaffordable.

She's now back home in Reykjavík, out of work, her entire
Plan A for her future abandoned. "What angers me most
about our former government here," she says now, "is that
they didn't have the decency to be ashamed."

That's what can happen when a country's banks go bad.
Some of the detail of the Icelandic case is exotic: basically,
a small group of rich and powerful people sold assets back
and forth to one another and created a grotesque bubble of
phony wealth. "Thirty or forty people did this, and the
whole country is paying for it," a Reykjavík cab driver told
me—and I've yet to meet an Icelander who disagrees. But
although a small group of people was ultimately responsible for the bubble, the whole country was caught up in it,
as a huge wave of cheap credit lifted Iceland into a kind of
economic fantasyland. The banks were at the heart of this
process. Iceland's banks had been state-owned until 2001,
when the economically liberal Independence Party privatized them. The result was explosive growth—fake growth,
but explosive. A country with 300,000 people—the population of Tampa, Florida—and no natural resources except
thermal energy and fish stocks suddenly developed a huge
banking sector whose assets were twelve times bigger than
the whole of the economy. There should have been a warning sign in the coinage, which is based on fish: the 1-króna
piece bears a salmon, the 10 krónur a school of capelin, the
50 krónur coin a crab, the 100 krónur a plaice. Thumbing
the coins, you think: these guys know a lot about fish;
about banking, maybe not so much.

But no one paid any attention to that. Credit was so
cheap it seemed effectively free. I spoke to Valgarður Bragason, a mason, who bought two houses and a plot of land,
taking out three different mortgages to the tune of about
$750,000, on the basis of conversations with the bank

which never lasted more than fifteen minutes. One of the loans was denominated not in Icelandic krónur, which had high interest rates, but in a basket of five different foreign currencies. This might sound like a crazy thing to have done—but in Iceland and elsewhere, in the early years of the new century, the normal rules of personal finance had been suspended. Yes, many consumers and borrowers were personally irresponsible; but then, they were encouraged to be. The banks treated financial irresponsibility as a valuable commodity, almost as a natural resource, to be lovingly groomed and cultivated. Cheap credit was everywhere: cold calls from lenders and letters with precompleted credit card applications arrived nearly daily, and when I phoned my own bank, Barclays, before I was offered the option to get my account details or talk to anyone, a prerecorded message invited me to take out a new loan. Borrowers were urged to gorge on cheap credit, like geese being stuffed to create foie gras. "I was trying to be cautious," one friend told me, "but my financial adviser said, it's like when the road is clear ahead of you, it's just silly not to put your foot down. So I put my foot down." Him and millions of others.

For a while, Iceland looked like a modern economic miracle. Then reality intruded, and the Icelandic economy crashed in the same manner in which Mike Campbell went broke in *The Sun Also Rises*: "two ways, gradually then suddenly." A slow decline in the króna in early 2008 was made much worse by the fact that so many Icelanders had those foreign-currency loans: 40,500 of them, in fact, to a total value of 115 billion krónur, about £30,000 each at the time. (Most of this money seems to have been spent on fancy cars.) Forty thousand people is a lot of people in a country with a population of only three hundred thousand. They were grievously exposed by the decline in value of the

króna, because when the króna went south, the cost of
their loans went violently north. The first nine months of
2008 were a financial bad dream, one which abruptly and
irrevocably became real when, on October 6, the prime
minister of Iceland, Geir Haarde, went on television to tell
people, convolutedly and without accepting any responsibility, that the country was effectively bankrupt. The banks
were closing and all Iceland's foreign reserves were frozen,
except for vital needs such as food, fuel, and medicine. And
that's what left Rakel Stefánsdóttir and hundreds like her
standing in the street, frowning at their bank cards and
wondering why they seemed so suddenly to have run out of
cash. It's just as well none of them yet knew the real picture. Iceland's banks had grown so big so fast that the
banking system was, in a much-used phrase, "an elephant
balancing on a mouse's back." The banks' overseas assets
were frozen, a process which began when the U.K. government used antiterrorist legislation to prevent the movement
of Icelandic banks' money out of the country. Icelanders
are still cross about that: in Reykjavík I came across a
T-shirt with a picture of the British prime minister and the
slogan "Brown is the color of poo." A bit harsh. But they're
entitled to be angry with somebody, because the implosion
of Iceland's banks left them exposed to losses of £116,000
for every man, woman, and child in the country.

How did we get here? How did we get from an economy in which banks and credit function the way they are
supposed to, to this place we're in now, the Reykjavíkiza-
tion of the world economy? The crisis was based on a problem, a mistake, a failure, and a culture; but before it was
any of those things, it arose from a climate—and the climate was that which followed the capitalist world's victory
over communism and the fall of the Berlin Wall.

This was especially apparent to me because I grew up in Hong Kong at the time when it was the most unbridled free-market economy in the world. Hong Kong was the economic Wild West. There were no rules, no income taxes (well, eventually there was a top tax of 15 percent), no welfare state, no guarantee of health care or schooling. Shantytowns sprawled halfway up the hillsides of Hong Kong island; the inhabitants of those shanties had no electricity or running water or medicine or education for their children. Completely unregulated sweatshop factories were a significant part of the colony's economy. The ugly edge of no-rules capitalism was everywhere apparent. But the ways in which that same capitalism created growth and wealth were everywhere apparent too—and it was impossible not to notice that this devil-take-the-hindmost free-for-all system was something people were risking their lives to try. Refugees from Communist China swam, crawled, and smuggled themselves into Hong Kong in every imaginable way, and they regularly died in the attempt. If they did get across the border, the rule was that they were sent back when caught, unless they got as far as Boundary Street in Kowloon, at which point they had the right to remain. There was something horribly vivid about that rule, like a grown-up version of a child's game: get to Home, and you're safe. Otherwise, back to tyranny. But there was no mistaking the way Hong Kong shone as a place of hope and opportunity to the people who were trying to get there—and the realization that what they were trying to get to wasn't the place so much as the system. The land and people were the same; only the system was different. So the system must be something of extraordinary power. Even a child could see that. You could see it mainly in the sheer speed of change. It was a regular event to go round a corner and experience the jolt of not knowing where the hell you were, because some regular landmark had disappeared. And as for Communist China, prior to its opening up to travelers from 1979, that was a subject of fear and wonder and legend. It was something visitors were always taken to see, the farthest point in the New Territories, from which you could look out into China. On the Hong Kong side was a Gurkha observation post on a hill. You looked out into paddy fields, a river, and not much else. Now go and stand on the same spot today, and you are looking at Shenzhen, the fastest-growing city in China, with a population of 9 million—in a place where there were literally no buildings thirty years ago.

At that time, Hong Kong was like an experiment, a lab test in free-market capitalism. Circumstances of history and demographics had conspired to make it a global one-off. Britain, in particular, seemed much slower, more cautious, more regulated, warier of change. But in the three decades after I left Hong Kong, it was as if there had been a kind of reverse takeover, in which Hong Kong's rules took over the rest of the world. Instead of being a special case, the unbridled and unregulated operation of the free market became the new normal. It wasn't so much that this version of capitalism won the argument as that it won by sheer force: countries which had adopted it were growing their economies faster than those that weren't. You can't accurately measure subjective changes in the texture of people's experiences, but you can measure growth in GDP, and the evidence from GDP was irrefutable. With Ronald Reagan in power in the United States and Margaret Thatcher in power in the United Kingdom, a Hong Kong-ite version of free-market capitalism took over the world. I couldn't go home again, but in some important respects it made no difference, because home was coming to me.

The version of capitalism which spread so thoroughly around the world had its ideological underpinnings from Adam Smith, via Friedrich von Hayek and Milton Friedman, and tended to act as if there were a fundamental connection between capitalism and democracy. Subsequent events, I believe, have shown that to be untrue—but that's a whole argument, a whole different book in itself. Suffice it to say that this version of capitalism, often dubbed the Anglo-Saxon model, spread around the world.* The formula involved liberalization of markets, deregulation of the economy and especially the financial sector, privatization of state assets, low taxes, and the lowest possible amount of state spending. The state's role was seen as being to get out of the way of the wealth-creating power of individuals and companies. The United States and the United Kingdom were the global cheerleaders for these policies, and their success in growing their GDP led to their adoption in amended forms in New Zealand, Australia, Ireland, Spain (to an extent), Iceland, Russia, Poland, and elsewhere. A version of these policies is imposed by the IMF when it goes into countries which need financial assistance. Measurable growths in GDP tend to follow the adoption of these policies; so do measurable growths in inequality.

For Marxists, and for a certain kind of anticorporatist, antiglobalizing voice on the left, this kind of capitalism "sowed the seeds of its own destruction." Marx's argument in using that phrase was that as workers were increasingly brought together in factories, they would have increasing

---

*I use the term "Anglo-Saxon" in this book, because it's standard terminology, but it is in fact a horribly misleading term, because so many of the people advocating and pursuing the free-market policies aren't, in point of fact, Anglo-Saxon at all. "Anglo-American" would be more accurate, but it hasn't caught on.

opportunities to observe how they were exploited and also to organize against that exploitation. A more modern view would be that free-market capitalism has an inherent propensity for inequality and for cycles of boom and bust—there's an extensive body of work studying these cycles. We can note that, in the current case, the practice fit the theory. The biggest boom in seventy years turned straight into the biggest bust. The rest of this book tells the story of how that happened, but there was one essential precursor to all the subsequent events, without which the explosion and implosion would not have occurred in the form they did: and that was the fall of the Berlin wall, the collapse of the Soviet Union, and the end of the Cold War.

Explicit arguments about the conflict between the West and the Communist bloc were never especially profitable. The camps were too entrenched; the larger philosophical issues tended to be boiled off until nothing but the residue of party politics remained. On the right, it was so obvious that the Communist regimes were mass-murdering prison states that there was nothing further of profit to be discussed. On the left, it was equally clear that capitalism had its own long list of crimes to its name; that it would always make a fetish of capital ahead of the interests of human beings; and that by contrast the socialist countries were at least thinking about, or acting out the possibility of, alternatives to that model, even if they were doing it wrong. But I've always felt that both schools of thought missed a critical point. The socialist bloc countries had grave, irredeemable flaws; the Western liberal democracies are the most admirable societies that have ever existed. There is no "moral equivalence," as it used to be called, between them. However—and this is the uncomfortable move in the argument, the one which outrages both the old Right and the old Left—the population of the West benefited from the existence, the policies, and the example of the socialist bloc. For decades there was the equivalent of an ideological beauty contest between the capitalist West and the Communist East, both of them vying to look as if they offered their citizens the better, fairer way of life. The result in the East was oppression; the result in the West was free schooling, universal health care, weeks of paid holiday, and a consistent, across-the-board rise in opportunities and rights. In Western Europe, the existence of local parties with a strong and explicit admiration for the socialist model created a powerful impetus to show that ordinary people's lives were better under capitalist democracy. In America, the equivalent pressures were far fainter—which is why American workers have, to Europeans, grotesquely limited vacation time (two weeks a year), no free health care, and a life expectancy lower than that of Europe.

And then the good guys won, the beauty contest came to an end, and the decades of Western progress in relation to equality and individual rights came to an end. In the United States, the median income—the number bang in the middle of the earnings curve—has for workers stayed effectively unchanged since the 1970s, while inequality of income between the top and the bottom has risen sharply. Since 1970, the income of the highest-paid fifth of U.S. earners has grown 60 percent. Everyone else is paid 10 percent less.[2] In the 1970s, Americans and Europeans worked about the same amount of hours per year; now Americans work almost twice as much.[3] That's the case for the people in the middle: for the people at the top, and especially for the people at the very top, it's different: between 1980 and 2007, the richest 0.1 percent of Americans saw their income grow by 700 percent.[4]

Here's a way of thinking about the change since the fall of the Wall. One of the most vivid consequences was the abolition of the ban on torture, which had previously been a defining characteristic of the democratic world's self-definition. Previously, when the West did bad things, it chose to deny having done them or did them under the cover of darkness or had proxies do them on their behalf. In other words, corrupt regimes linked to the West might commit crimes such as torture and imprisonment without due process, but when the crimes came to light, the relevant governments did everything they could to deny and cover up the charges—the crimes were considered to be shameful things. With the end of the ideological beauty contest, that changed. Consider the issue of waterboarding. At the Tokyo Tribunal it was an indictable offense: a Japanese officer, Yukio Asano, was sentenced to fifteen years' hard labor for waterboarding a U.S. civilian. During the Vietnam War, U.S. forces would occasionally use waterboarding—but when they were found out, there was a scandal. In January 1968, *The Washington Post* ran a photograph of an American soldier waterboarding a North Vietnamese captive: there was an uproar, and he was court-martialed. With the end of the Cold War and the beginning of the "war on terror," waterboarding became an explicitly endorsed tool of U.S. security. (And British security too, by extension.) At the time when the democratic world was preoccupied by demonstrating its moral superiority to the Communist bloc, that would never have happened.

The same goes for the way in which the financial sector was allowed to run out of control. It was a series of events which took place not in a vacuum but in a climate. That climate was one of unchallenged victory for the capitalist system, a clear ideological hegemony of a type which had never existed before: it was the first moment when capitalism was unchallenged as the world's dominant political-economic system. Under those circumstances, it could have been predicted that the financial sector, which presides over the operation of capitalism, was in a position to begin rewarding itself with a disproportionate piece of the economic pie. There was no global antagonist to point at and jeer at the rise in the number and size of the fat cats; there was no embarrassment about allowing the rich to get so much richer so very quickly. With the financial sector's direct ownership of capitalism, great fortunes began to be made by employees doing nothing other than their jobs—which, in the case of bankers, involve taking on risks, usually with other people's money. To make more money and earn more bonuses (which usually constitute 60 percent of an investment banker's pay) is simple: you just take on more risk. The upside is the upside, and the downside—well, it increasingly came to seem that for the bankers themselves, there wasn't one. In a brilliant piece in *The Atlantic* called "The Quiet Coup," Simon Johnson, the former chief economist at the International Monetary Fund—and therefore a man whose former job involved knocking heads together in self-bankrupted kleptocracies—explained that this process was a vital part of "how the U.S. became a banana republic."

The financial industry has not always enjoyed such favored treatment. But for the past twenty-five years or so, finance has boomed, becoming ever more powerful. The boom began with the Reagan years, and it only gained strength with the deregulatory policies of the Bill Clinton and George W. Bush administrations. Several other factors helped fuel the financial industry's ascent. Paul Volcker's monetary policy in the 1980s, and the increased volatility in interest rates that accompanied it, made bond trading much more lucrative. The invention of securitization, interest rate swaps, and credit default swaps greatly increased the volume of transactions that bankers could make money on. And the aging and increasingly wealthy population invested more and more money in securities, helped by the invention of the IRA and the 401(k) plan. Together, these developments vastly increased the profit opportunities in financial services.

Not surprisingly, Wall Street ran with these opportunities. From 1973 to 1985, the financial sector never earned more than 16 percent of domestic corporate profits. In 1986, that figure reached 19 percent. In the 1990s, it oscillated between 21 percent and 30 percent, higher than it had ever been in the postwar period. This decade, it reached 41 percent. Pay rose just as dramatically. From 1948 to 1982, average compensation in the financial sector ranged between 99 percent and 108 percent of the average for all domestic private industries. From 1983, it shot upward, reaching 181 percent in 2007.

The great wealth that the financial sector created and concentrated gave bankers enormous political weight—a weight not seen in the United States since the era of J. P. Morgan (the man). In that period, the banking panic of 1907 could be stopped only by coordination among private-sector bankers: no government entity was able to offer an effective response. But that first age of banking oligarchs came to an

end with the passage of significant banking regulation in response to the Great Depression; the reemer-
gence of an American financial oligarchy is quite
recent.[5]

Accompanying this increase in wealth has been an increase in political muscle. The rich are always listened to
more than the poor, but that's now especially true since,
with the end of the Cold War, there is so much less political
capital in the idea of equality and fairness. The free market stopped being one way of arranging the world, subject
to argument and comparison with other systems: it became
an item of faith, a near-mystical belief. In that belief system, the finance industry made up the class of priests and
magicians and began to be treated as such. In the United
Kingdom, that meant a kind of ideological hegemony for
the City of London. The government adopted City models of behavior and the vocabulary to go with them—the
language of targets and goals being a sign of uncritical and
uninformed governmental Cityphilia. David Kynaston, the
author of a magisterial four-volume history of the City of
London, comes in his fourth book to discuss "City cultural
supremacy" and concludes that "in all sorts of ways (short-
term performance, shareholder value, league tables) and in
all sorts of areas (education, the NHS and the BBC, to name
but three), bottom-line City imperatives had been trans-
planted wholesale into British society."[6] Successive governments gave the City more or less everything it wanted. This
process began with Margaret Thatcher's election in 1979:
one of the incoming government's first actions, practically
as well as symbolically important, was the abolition of exchange controls, which opened the United Kingdom to the
international flow of capital. Subsequent legislation carried

on the trend, culminating in the "Big Bang" of 1986. This was the moment in which a deregulatory process which could have taken years or decades was packed into a single act: in effect (and for the purposes of simplification), all the historic barriers, separations, and rules demarcating different areas of banking and finance and participation in the stock market were simultaneously abolished. I have used the word "bank" throughout this book to simplify the point, but in reality many modern financial intermediaries—the bodies standing in between the people who want to borrow money and the people who want to lend it—aren't, strictly speaking, banks at all. There are home loan specialists, credit unions, private equity funds, securitization specialists, money market funds, hedge funds, and insurance companies, all of them differently regulated and not a few of them functioning as separate parts of the same institution. The institutions which make up this world of nonbank banks are sometimes referred to collectively as the "shadow banking system," and insofar as it has a capital, that capital is the City of London.

Taken together, what this led to was the City's increasing dominance of British economic life—and Wall Street's equivalent domination in the United States. This, in turn, makes it all the more striking how little knowledge most people have of what goes on in the City and the Street—what it is for, what it does, and how it affects their everyday life. Even very well informed citizens tend not to realize just what a force in the world the bond market is, a fact reflected in the famous observation by James Carville in the early years of President Clinton's first administration: "I used to think if there was reincarnation, I wanted to come back as the president or the pope or a .400 baseball hitter. But now I want to come back as the bond market. You can intimidate everybody." But the ordinary elector knows almost nothing about how these markets work and the impact they have. David Kynaston points out that under communism, children from primary school upward were taught the principles and practice of the system and were thoroughly drilled in how it was supposed to work. There is nothing comparable to that in the capitalist world. The City is, in terms of its basic functioning, a far-off country of which we know little.

This climate of thinking informed all subsequent events. With the fall of the Berlin Wall, capitalism began a victory party that ran for almost two decades. Capitalism is not inherently fair: it does not, in and of itself, distribute the rewards of economic growth equitably. Instead it runs on the bases of winner take all and to them that hath shall be given. For several decades after the Second World War, the Western liberal democracies devoted themselves to the question of how to harness capitalism's potential for economic growth to the political imperative to provide better lives for ordinary people. The jet engine of capitalism was harnessed to the oxcart of social justice, to much bleating from the advocates of pure capitalism, but with the effect that the Western liberal democracies became the most admirable societies that the world has ever seen. Not the most admirable we can imagine, and not perfect; but the best humanity had as yet been able to achieve. Then the Wall came down, and, to various extents, the governments of the West began to abandon the social justice aspect of the general postwar project. The jet engine was unhooked from the oxcart and allowed to roar off at its own speed. The result was an unprecedented boom, which had two big things wrong with it: it wasn't fair, and it wasn't sustainable. This phenomenon was especially clear in Iceland, because the country privatized its banks only in 2001. The collectivist tradition in Iceland is so strong that it is more like a fact of national character than like an ideology—and this doesn't seem inappropriate in a country very aware of its isolation, its history as a Viking settlement, and the always-apparent inhospitability of the geography and climate. In the 1980s, however, the Independence Party, which had been more or less permanently in power since Iceland became independent from Denmark, began to adopt a more ideological turn. Its younger and more energetic politicians looked admiringly at the free-market policies being adopted by Ronald Reagan and Margaret Thatcher and began to wonder what Iceland might be capable of if it were freed from the current model of nationalization and regulation. A long march toward the free market began, and in 2001 the banks were privatized, a policy which was a triumphant success—until it turned into a total disaster.

That's how fast, and how completely, things can go wrong for a society if its banks go bad. This is because banks are central to the operation of a developed economy; in particular, they are central to the creation of credit, and credit is as important to the modern economy as oxygen is to human beings. When the banks go wrong, everything goes wrong: a bank crisis gives you that slamming-the-car-into-reverse feeling.

This is how it's supposed to work. A well-run bank is a machine for making money. The basic principle of banking is to pay a low rate of interest to the people who lend money and charge a higher rate to the people who borrow it. The bank borrows at 3 percent (say), and lends at 6 percent, and as long as it keeps the two amounts in line and makes sure that it lends money only to people who will be able to pay it back, it will reliably make money forever.

This institution, in and of itself, will generate activity in the rest of the economy. The process is explained in Philip Coggan's excellent primer on the City, *The Money Machine: How the City Works*. Imagine, for the purpose of keeping things simple, a country with only one bank. A customer goes into the bank and deposits $200. Now the bank has $200 to invest, so it goes out and buys some shares with the money—not the full $200, but the amount minus the percentage it deems prudent to keep in cash, just in case any depositors come and make a withdrawal. That amount, called the "cash ratio," is set by the government: in this example, let's say it's 20 percent. So our bank goes out and buys $160 of shares from, say, You Inc. Then You Inc. goes and deposits its $160 in the bank; so now the bank has $360 of deposits, of which it needs to keep only 20 percent—$72—in cash: so now it can go out and buy another $128 of shares in You Inc., raising its total holding in You Inc. to $288. Once again, You Inc. goes and deposits the money in the bank, which goes out again and buys more shares, and on the process goes. The only thing imposing a limit is the need to keep 20 percent in cash, so the depositing-and-buying cycle ends when the bank has $200 in cash and $800 in You Inc. shares; it also has $1,000 of customer deposits, the initial $200 plus all the money from the share transactions. The initial $200 has generated a balance sheet of $1,000 in assets and $1,000 in liabilities. Magic!

This aspect of how banks work is critical to the way the economy works; it's the reason banks are not just some convenient add-on to capitalism but are at the center of how it's supposed to work. Banks create credit, and credit makes the economy work. In a sense, credit isn't just an aspect of the economy, it *is* the economy—the seamless, ceaseless, frictionless, ebb and flow and circulation of credit. When it works, this process is a wonder of the world.

In this system, the recording of the movement of money is indispensable and has a history of its own. The central invention in this history are the financial statements, of which the most important, in this story, is the balance sheet. We don't know who invented balance sheets; they seem to have been in use in Venice as early as the thirteenth century. But we do know who wrote down the method behind them and in the process invented modern accounting, which relies on four financial statements to provide a full picture of any given business: the balance sheet, the income statement, the cash flow statement, and the statement of retained earnings. The man who wrote down the method for gathering and recording the relevant information was Luca Pacioli, a Franciscan monk and friend of both Piero della Francesca and Leonardo da Vinci, whose assistant he was for many years. Pacioli wrote *Summa de Arithmetica*, the book which laid out the method of double-entry bookkeeping which is still in use in more or less every business in the world. (He also wrote about magic, in the sense of conjuring. I'd like to think he would have enjoyed the old joke about accountants: "What's two plus two?" "What would you like it to be?") There's something amazing about the fact that a method used in Venice in the thirteenth century and written down in Tuscany in the fifteenth should still be in daily use in every financial enterprise in the developed world.

Of the four financial statements, the balance sheet is the one which provides a glimpse into a moment of time. The others show processes, flows of money; the balance sheet is a snapshot. A balance sheet is divided into Assets on the left and Liabilities on the right. Assets are things which belong to you, liabilities are things which belong to other people. Here's what an individual's balance sheet might look like:

ASSETS
House	$200,000
Deposits in bank	$10,000
Car	$10,000
Stuff I own	$15,000
Money people owe me	$5,000
Pension	$40,000
Total	$280,000

LIABILITIES
Share of house owned by bank	$130,000
Credit card debt	$2,000
Car loan	$2,000
Unpaid debt on stuff I own	$6,000
Total	$140,000
Equity	$140,000
Total liabilities and equity	$280,000

You'll notice there is something mysterious on there called "Equity." This is the magic ingredient that makes a balance sheet always balance: it is added to your liabilities so that they match your assets. The fact that it appears on the Liability side of the column might make equity seem sinister, but it isn't: it's a good thing. It's the amount by which you are in the clear; it's the amount by which your assets exceed your liabilities. Your equity is your safety margin; it is your net worth, it is the thing which keeps you in business.

Now imagine for a moment that you are a business: you are now You Inc. You set out to sell shares in yourself. The part of you that you sell shares in is the equity. The buyer is taking over not the assets and liabilities but the equity. Say I buy 10 percent of your equity, as set out in the balance sheet above, at a price of $14,000 (an accurate price, since that's exactly what it's worth today). In a year's time, say you've paid back $10,000 of your mortgage, your house price has gone up by half, you're being paid better at work, and so you have another $10,000 in the bank—golly, our equity is now $190,000. My one-tenth share of your equity is now worth $19,000. Cool. I could sell my share in your equity and make a nice profit, or I could just sit on it, betting that you would do even better in the future. On the other, scarier hand, you could have had a lousy year: your house price has halved, you have been put on part-time work so your salary has halved and wiped out your savings, various of your debtors have gone bankrupt, your car has lost 30 percent of its value, your pension has been wiped out by bad investments: in sum, your assets have gone down by $160,000. Your liabilities, on the other hand, are the same. There's a problem: your liabilities now exceed your assets by a cool $20,000. In plain English, you're broke. In the language of accountancy, you are insolvent. You have met one of the two criteria for insolvency: your liabilities are greater than your assets. The other criterion is the inability to meet your debts as they fall due. In British law, meeting either criterion makes you insolvent. It is a criminal offense to trade while insolvent.

There may be a loophole, however. Are you really insolvent? I've made things clear cut for the purposes of this example, but you could argue—and in comparable cases people do—that your problem is not so much insolvency as illiquidity. Liquidity is the ability to turn assets into something that can be bought or sold. In a depressed housing market, the problem with your house could easily be not so much its value as the fact that you can't sell it because nobody is buying property at the moment. Or rather, you can sell it, but you have to do so for an artificially depressed, crazy-cheap price: a "fire sale" price. When the market returns to normal, you will be able to sell your house for its true value, so you aren't really insolvent, you're just caught in a "liquidity trap." In practice, all you would do in the above example—as long as you weren't really You Inc., in which case you might well be under a legal obligation to go into receivership—would be to simply ignore the question and keep going. You'd hope to be able to pay your bills as they fell due and hang on for grim life until your house price recovered. As we speak, hundreds of thousands of people across the United Kingdom—around the world—are doing precisely that. The current estimate of the number of people in the United Kingdom with "negative equity" is 900,000.

A business can't have negative equity; if it does, it is insolvent. But businesses can and do have considerably different levels of equity, and it often makes their businesses look different in an instantly recognizable, at-a-glance way. At business school, they play a game—sorry, "undertake an exercise"—in which students are given balance sheets and asked to determine what type of business the company is in. What's this business?

	GROUP		COMPANY	
	2007 £m	2006 £m	2007 £m	2006 £m
ASSETS				
Cash and balances at central banks	17,866	6,121	—	—
Treasury and other eligible bills subject to repurchase agreements	7,090	1,426	—	—

(continued)

I.O.U.

	GROUP		COMPANY	
	2007 £m	2006 £m	2007 £m	2006 £m
ASSETS				
Other treasury and other eligible bills	11,139	4,065	—	—
Treasury and other eligible bills	18,229	5,491	—	—
Loans and advances to banks	219,460	82,606	7,686	7,252
Loans and advances to customers	829,250	466,893	307	286
Debt securities subject to repurchase agreements	100,561	58,874	—	—
Other debt securities	175,866	68,377	—	—
Debt securities	276,427	127,251	—	—
Equity shares	53.026	13.504	—	—
Investments in Group undertakings	—	—	43,542	21,784
Settlement balances	16,589	7,425	—	—
Derivatives	337,410	116,681	173	—
Intangible assets	48,492	18,904	—	—
Property, plant and equipment	18,750	18,420	—	—
Prepayments, accrued income and other assets	19,066	8,136	127	3
Assets of disposal groups	45,954	—	—	—
TOTAL ASSETS	1,900,519	871,432	51,835	29,325

LIABILITIES				
Deposits by banks	312,633	132,143	5,572	738
Customer accounts	682,365	384,222	—	—
Debt securities in issue	273,615	85,963	13,453	2,139
Settlement balances and short positions	91,021	49,476	—	—
Derivatives	332,060	118,112	179	42
Accruals, deferred income and other liabilities	34,024	15,660	8	15
Retirement benefit liabilities	496	1,992	—	—
Deferred taxation	5,510	3,264	3	—
Insurance liabilities	10,162	7,456	—	—
Subordinated liabilities	37,979	27,654	7,743	8,194
Liabilities of disposal groups	29,228	—	—	—
Total liabilities	1,809,093	825,942	26,958	11,128
Minority interests	38,388	5,263	—	—
Equity owners	53,038	40,227	24,877	18,197
TOTAL EQUITY	91,426	45,490	24,877	18,197
TOTAL LIABILITIES AND EQUITY	1,900,519	871,432	51,835	29,325

Our business school chums will have no trouble working this one out: from the huge levels of assets and liabilities and the fact that the main category of liabilities is customer deposits, it will be immediately apparent that this business is a bank. If they've been swotting up, they may even be able to work out which bank it is, since a clue is in the figure for "total assets": £1,900,519,000,000. One point nine trillion pounds. Since the entire GDP of the United Kingdom is £1.7 trillion, this is a freakishly large bank. Any guesses? Okay, this is the Royal Bank of Scotland. RBS was in 2008, by the size of its assets, not just a big bank and not just one of the biggest companies in Europe. The Royal Bank of Scotland, by asset size, was the biggest company in the world. If I had to pick a single fact which summed up the cultural gap between the City of London and the rest of the country, it would be that one. I have yet to meet a single person not employed in financial services who was aware of it; I wasn't aware of it myself. We're all well aware of it now, though, since the British taxpayer has had to bail out RBS to the tune of tens of billions of pounds: no one yet knows how much the final cost will be, but £100 billion is probably not far off the mark, and it could easily be much more.

It seems weird, at first glance and indeed at second glance, that bank balance sheets list customer deposits as liabilities, but it makes sense if you think about it, since a liability is at heart something that belongs to somebody else, and the customers' deposits belong to the customers. This was something that my father, who worked for a bank, used often to say to me: don't forget that if you have money in a bank account, you're lending the bank money. Banks themselves certainly don't forget it. Actually, that's not true. They forget it all the time in their dealings with their customer/creditors—us. They act as if it's their money and they are doing us a favor by letting it sit in their bank earning interest. A spectacular example of this, in modern Britain, is the question of the check-clearing system. If I give you a check today and you pay it into your bank, the funds will clear out of my account tomorrow but won't be credited to your account until three days later—if you're lucky; it can take up to seven days. This is much too slow; but it's okay because a government report, commissioned by Gordon Brown, has made stinging criticisms of the payment system and action has been promised. Cool! But wait! The report was published, and the promise of decisive action was made, in 2000, when Brown was chancellor of the Exchequer. Legislation and new regulatory bodies to enforce it have repeatedly been promised, but the problem has consistently been the industry's reluctance to act, since this is change which does nothing to benefit banks' profits—it benefits only customers. The banks just can't get excited about it, especially since this reform offers a pure bonus to customers, with no extra revenues to be extracted in the process. Change was supposed to have finally begun being "rolled out" to customers in May 2008. Speaking for myself, it's had no effect at all. Ten years after the check-clearing system was declared a national scandal, checks paid into my account still take at least three days to clear. This is the reality of how the banks view their customers in their daily dealings.[7]

Take a look at the balance sheet, however, and at the page after page of corporate reports and footnotes which accompany it, and it's a different story. There, the depositors hold all the power. High levels of deposits means high levels of liabilities; and high levels of liabilities oblige a bank to have high levels of assets. Since banks are mainly in the business of lending money, high levels of assets mean high levels of loans. That means that a bank's main assets are other people's debts. This is another distinctive feature of bank balance sheets, the fact that its principal assets are other people's debts to it.

The balance sheets of other businesses look very different. They're smaller, for a start: only banks are this bloated with assets and liabilities. That's natural, since the business model of banking, involving lots of money coming in and sitting in accounts, balanced by lots of lending, is always going to involve big sums on the balance sheet and relatively small amounts of equity. A company with a quicker turnover will look very different. Apple, for instance, in 2008 had $39.5 billion in assets, $18.5 billion in liabilities, and $21 billion in equity; compare that to RBS's £1,900 billion, £1,809 billion, and £91 billion. Apple's assets are a fiftieth the size of RBS, but its equity is bigger than its liabilities. In that sense, Apple is a safer business than RBS; it has a larger safety cushion, a proportionately bigger margin for error. Of course, it might be that it has a bigger margin for error because it is an inherently riskier business. Banking should be much more solid than computers/gadgets/music, but the fact that banks will always have elephantine balance sheets in proportion to their equity means they have a tendency to be a little less secure than they look at first glance. That's one of the many reasons why banks are, in their corporate body language, so keen to look as imposing and rocklike as they possibly can.

Apple's accounts are all about how many computers, phones, and songs the company can sell, since its financial health depends on those. (Apple's iTunes is the biggest music retailer in both the United Kingdom and United States.) RBS's accounts are all about its loans, since the financial health of the company depends on the quality of those loans. It follows from that that RBS's accounts are all about loan risk, since the profitability of the loans depends on how likely they are to be repaid. For that reason the nature of the assets—the loans—is all-important, and risk is not some marginal factor but the core of a bank's business. Risk is always an important issue for any company, but for a bank, it isn't just important, it's its whole business. Banking does not just involve the management of risk; banking *is* the management of risk.

A big component of that risk is how big to be. In practice, that means how much bigger your liabilities can be than your equity. This is known as your "leverage," and it is usually expressed as a multiple, the amount by which you have to multiply your equity to make it equal your liabilities. In the personal finance balance sheet given above, your equity is $140,000 and your liabilities are $140,000, so your leverage ratio is 1 to 1. That's nice and safe—but it's very different from the position of Britain's banks. This has turned out to be a gigantic problem for Britain, because our big banks aren't just big, they're huge: the four biggest each has a capital value of more than a trillion pounds. They are highly leveraged, too. The ratio of Barclays' assets to its equity at its 2008 peak was 61.3 to 1. Because the liabilities match the assets plus the equities, that means that the liabilities are colossal. Imagine that for a moment translated to your own finances, so that you could stretch what you actually, unequivocally own to borrow more than sixty times the amount. (I'd buy an island. What about you?) During the boom, the leverage ratios of the big European banks—the multiple by which their assets exceeded their equity—reached a point where they were the financial equivalent of bungee jumping: even though everyone tells you it's supposed to be safe, you still have to be an adrenaline addict to risk it. These were the ratios for the big European banks on June 30, 2008, when the financial tsunami was just about to hit: UBS, 46.9 to 1; ING Group, 48.8 to 1; HSBC Holding, 20.1 to 1; Barclays Bank, 61.3 to 1; Deutsche Bank, 52.5 to 1; Fortis, 33.3 to 1; Lloyds TSB, 34.1 to 1; RBS, 18.8 to 1; Crédit Agricole, 40.5 to 1; BNP Paribas, 36.1 to 1; Credit Suisse, 33.4 to 1.[8]

The figures for the big American banks aren't quite as bad, but they're bad enough: what they boil down to is median leverage ratios of 35 to 1 in the United States and 45 to 1 in Europe. Another way of looking at these ratios is to say that they represent the amount of the bank's assets which have to go bad for the bank to be insolvent. In the United States, on average, if $\frac{1}{35}$th of the bank's assets go bad, the bank is bust; in the European Union, $\frac{1}{45}$ of bad assets would have the same effect. This is, obviously, a highly precarious position. It was also no accident, because those risks were also the reason why the banks had a boom period. The banks were incredibly profitable not because they were doing anything better but simply because they were making bigger, riskier bets—plunking down more money on the roulette wheel. This isn't just a metaphor, it's the actual conclusion of an academic study made by Andrew Haldane, the Bank of England's executive in charge of financial stability. Between 1986 and 2006, the average annual return on banking shares rocketed from its historic norm of 2 percent to 16 percent. Why? Because the banks were making bigger bets. There was no skill, efficiency, intelligence, or judgment involved, just riskier bets. In Haldane's exact words, "Since 2000, rising leverage fully accounts for movements in UK banks' ROE [return on equity]—both the rise to around 24% in 2007 and the subsequent fall into negative territory in 2008."[9] This is astounding stuff. Haldane is in effect saying that most of those bankers paying themselves monster bonuses were doing so simply as a result of making bigger bets—and, as it turned out, it was we the taxpayers who, unwittingly and unwillingly, were bankrolling their ever-riskier wagers. This wasn't just looking for trouble, it was sending trouble a "save the date" card, followed by a formal invitation, followed by nagging e-mails and phone calls just to make absolutely sure.

What links all the banks which have hit trouble—and all the other companies and institutions around the world which have been felled by the credit crunch—is that those bets went bad. Gigantic holes appeared on the left-hand side of their balance sheets, where "Assets" are listed. That suddenly and immediately meant they were at risk from having their liabilities exceed their assets—that is, being insolvent. Those now-worthless assets are for the most part linked in one way or another to the collapse in property prices in the United States and elsewhere. They are often described as "toxic assets" or "troubled assets," as they're euphemistically known in the U.S. scheme to buy them from the banks: the Troubled Assets Relief Program, or TARP. But the term "toxic assets" is misleading. It makes me think of Superman intercepting a rocket-powered canister of vileness unleashed by some villain and deflecting it into space. The assets in question don't contain some magic property of poisonous money-juice. The thing that's toxic about them is their prices. As Stephanie Flanders of the BBC has said, it would be more accurate to call them "toxic prices"—it would at least be an aid to clearer thinking.

The definition is usually stated as follows: these are assets which can't be accurately priced and which therefore spread uncertainty and insecurity throughout the financial system. But that isn't quite right. It's true that some of the problematic mortgage-backed assets at the moment have no price because there is no market for them, and no one knows whether or not there ever will be such a market again. But many of these assets do in fact have prices; there are buyers out there willing to acquire them. That makes sense. Considering Lloyds-HBOS, for instance, it's obviously not true that every mortgage sold in recent years by Halifax is a dud, spreading poison through the company's balance sheet. That defies common sense. It's probably the case that the bulk of the company's mortgages, perhaps the overwhelming bulk of them, perhaps including many worrisome recent loans, are viable. People's houses might not be worth what they paid for them, but in most cases they're going to continue paying the mortgages anyway. There must be many comparable examples out there, of highly out-of-fashion mortgage-based investments which aren't as deeply in trouble as the markets currently think. It might make sense, if you were an experienced investor in those markets, to investigate the possibility of buying some of these investments at a bargain price. The problem is that the prices are, from the banks' point of view, too low. The buyers are willing to acquire them at, say, twenty or thirty cents to the dollar, so that an asset whose notional worth is $10 million—for example, a derivative tracing its value from subprime mortgages—might have someone willing to buy it for $2 or $3 million. For the bank, that price is too low. It isn't too low in the sense that the bank wants a higher price; it's too low in the sense that, if it accepts the valuation, it will have a gigantic hole on the left-hand side of the balance sheet. Its assets aren't worth what they're supposed to be, and the bank is no longer solvent.

That problem is global, both in its consequences and in

its incidence. In one form or another, balance sheet abysses of this sort are responsible for all the collapses we've seen. Perhaps we can experience a twinge of national pride at the thought that this planetwide problem began with Northern Rock, which in September 2007 experienced the single most dreaded event which can overtake any financial institution, not seen in Britain for more than a century: a bank run. So many people turned up in person to withdraw money that the bank ended up paying out 5 percent of its total assets, a cool £1 billion in cash. Perhaps we can also experience a twinge of nostalgia at the fact that at the time of its nationalization a few months later, the £25 billion Northern Rock bailout was the biggest sum any government anywhere in the world had ever given to a private company.

Such, such were the days . . . the really serious wave of bailouts and collapses began with Bear Stearns in March 2008 and then went to the next level with the "conservatorship" of Fannie Mae and Freddie Mac on September 7, the largest nationalization in the history of the world. It was followed eight days later by the largest bankruptcy in the history of the world, when the investment bank Lehman Brothers went into Chapter 11, the American form of receivership. The next day saw the biggest bailout of a private company in history, with the U.S. government taking a 79.9 percent share in the insurer AIG. Merrill Lynch, the bank whose symbol is the Wall Street "roaring bull," was taken over by Bank of America on September 14, 2008. On September 18 came news of the biggest bank merger— carefully not denominated a takeover—in British history: Lloyds was to buy HBOS, the largest mortgage lender in the United Kingdom, with 20 percent of the market. This deal trashed the market's opinion of Lloyds and led to its boss, Victor Blank, being forced out of his job. On September 21, Goldman Sachs, the world's biggest investment bank, and Morgan Stanley converted their legal status from investment banks to holding banks, a change which allowed them access to help from the Federal Reserve in return for a greatly increased level of government supervision. On September 28, the Luxembourgeois, Belgian, and Dutch governments nationalized the bank Fortis, the biggest private employer in Belgium, at a cost of £1.3 billion. On September 29, Bradford & Bingley was nationalized, at a cost of £41.3 billion, and its branch network sold off to the Spanish bank Santander. The German commercial property loan giant Hypo Real Estate was bailed out on October 5 at a cost of £50 billion. The Icelandic banking system collapsed the next day. During the weekend of October 11–12, the British banking system teetered on the point of collapse—"the only time in my career," a senior banker told me, "when I've felt genuinely frightened." That same weekend, RBS was in receipt of an emergency injection of government cash, to the tune of £20 billion—the first stage of its bailout.

Since then things have calmed down, with only the occasional bailout-ette to concern us, such as that of the U.S. car industry or the Dunfermline Building Society. Nonetheless, I guarantee that at this very moment, somewhere in the world, somebody at one of the big banks is sitting with his head in his hands, looking at the company's balance sheet and sweating over this very problem. This might especially be the case in Europe, where banks and governments have delayed the reckoning with bad assets and bank insolvency for as long as they can. If the global economic crisis can be reduced to one single phenomenon, it is this: the fact that nobody knows which banks are solvent. Because banks are crucial to the creation and operation of credit, a bank crisis leads directly to a credit crunch. It's also why the huge amounts of money being pumped into the banking sector by governments are tending not to do the thing they were supposed to do, that is, restart lending to businesses and consumers. That's because—and here we can have that very rare thing, a brief moment of sympathy for the banksters—the banks are being given two totally incompatible goals. One is to rebuild their balance sheets and recapitalize themselves so they're no longer at risk of going broke. The second is to keep lending money. They're being told to save and to keep spending at the same time. It's not possible, and in the circumstances it's no mystery why banks are hoarding every penny they can get and calling in every loan they can: they're doing it in order to "deleverage" and rebuild their capital as fast as possible.

But that is cataclysmically destructive for the rest of the economy. It works like this: Bank's assets shrink in value. Bank therefore loses equity, because its liabilities are worth the same but its assets are worth less. Bank therefore has to shrink its assets further and contract its lending, in order to stay solvent. But because the bank is so highly leveraged, it has to make a huge amount of lending go away in order to cover a relatively small amount of equity loss. It's easy to see that many of the banks described above have leverage ratios of more than 30 to 1. That means that if they lose $100 million in equity they have to contract their assets and make $3 billion of lending go away just to stay at the same leverage ratio. If they want their leverage to actually shrink—which in practice most of them both want to do and are being encouraged to do—they have to shrink their assets even faster. That means lending even less money to businesses and individuals. That, in turn, makes everything worse for the entire economy. As Charles Morris points out in his book *The Trillion Dollar Meltdown: Easy Money, High Rollers, and the Great Credit Crash,* a credit bubble is a special category of event: "We are accustomed to thinking of bubbles and crashes in terms of specific markets—like junk bonds, commercial real estate, and tech stocks. Overpriced assets are like poison mushrooms. You eat them, you get sick, you learn to avoid them. A credit bubble is different. Credit is the air that financial markets breathe, and when the air is poisoned, there's no place to hide."[10]

What the banks want to be able to do is what most of us would do in comparable circumstances. Indeed, it's what a good few of us, myself included, have done in the past, during previous busts in the property market. When that happens, you just wait. Perhaps some of us are in the dreaded position of having the famous "negative equity," as described above. In their case they can sell and take a loss, if they can afford to—or they can just wait. Carry on living, and wait for prices to recover, and even if they don't they still have somewhere to live. That's what the banks would like to do about their toxic prices: wait for them to become nontoxic. If they were forced to value their assets today for the prices they could get today—a practice known as "mark to market," which is supposedly enforced on most kinds of assets—some of them would be insolvent. Since the current valuations would irretrievably trash their balance sheets, they would prefer not to accept them.

The trouble is that banks are not households. If banks sit on their hands and wait for valuations to recover, the economy will grind to a halt. The flow of money will stop, and the recession will be even more severe than it is already certain to be. That's because a situation in which banks are insolvent but stay in business means that there are "zombie banks." A zombie bank is a bank which is dead—insolvent—but has a horrible sort of pseudolife because it is being allowed to keep trading by (usually) an overindulgent government. Zombie banks are not hypothetical: it was zombie banks, created by an overcozy relationship between banks and the state, which after 1989 turned the Japanese economy from a wonder of the world to a comatose onlooker at global growth. The economy can't recover until the zombies are killed. The West was very free with brutally direct advice to Japan during its slowdown: we told Japan to hurry up and get on with it and slay its zombies already. In the aftermath of the credit crunch, it turns out we're much, much slower to take our own advice. Even Lawrence Summers, one of the finger waggers in chief when he was President Clinton's Treasury secretary, has admitted as much: "It is easier to be for more radical solutions when one lives thousands of miles away than when it is one's own country."[11] Horror-film zombies are relatively easy to deal with: they don't have investors, they don't hire lobbyists, they don't donate to political parties, they can't pick up the phone and frighten senior politicians. Zombie banks have none of those constraints and are much more of a problem: a scarily big problem. And, unlike zombies, they actually exist.

TWO

ROCKET SCIENCE

Finance, like other forms of human behavior, underwent a change in the twentieth century, a shift equivalent to the emergence of modernism in the arts—a break with common sense, a turn toward self-referentiality and abstraction, and notions that couldn't be explained in workaday English. In poetry, this moment took place with the publication of *The Waste Land*. In classical music, it was, perhaps, the première of *The Rite of Spring*. Dance, architecture, painting—all had comparable moments. (One of my favorites is in jazz: the moment in "A Night in Tunisia" when Charlie Parker plays a saxophone break, which is like the arrival of modernism, right there, in real time. It's said that the first time he went off on his solo, the other musicians simply put down their instruments and stared.) The moment in finance came in 1973, with the publication of a paper in the *Journal of Political Economy* titled "The Pricing of Options and Corporate Liabilities," by Fischer Black and Myron Scholes.

Derivatives have a bad press at the moment, but it's important to acknowledge their role in the long history of man's attempt to understand, control, and make money from risk. The study of risk is a humanist project, an attempt to abolish the idea of incomprehensible fate and replace it with the rational, quantifiable study of chance.[1] Once upon a time, we were the playthings of fate, and the future was unknowable; but then, starting with philosophers and mathematicians such as Pierre de Fermat, Blaise Pascal, and Christiaan Huygens, humanity began to work out ways in which the future could be measured and assessed in terms of probabilities. Just as experimental science had its roots in alchemy, so the study of probability had its roots in gambling: the first investigations into risk grew out of the curiosity of gamblers. Chance, and risk, began to be things which could be managed. An essential tool in doing so would be the category of financial instruments called derivatives.

Derivatives themselves are a long-standing feature of financial markets. At their simplest, a farmer will agree to a price for his next harvest a few months in advance; and the right to buy this harvest is a derivative, which can itself be sold. The name comes from the fact that a derivative's value derives from the underlying products. Today, the simplest forms of derivatives are options and futures. An option gives you the right, but not the obligation, to either buy or sell something at a specified future date for a specified price. Example: You spend $500 on an option to buy a Ferrari for $50,000 in a year's time. When the year is up, the Ferrari is on sale for $60,000—so your option is now worth $10,000, because that's how much money you can make by exercising the option, that is, buying the car and then selling it for its current price. Conversely, if in a year's time the Ferrari is on sale for $40,000, exercising your option would leave you out of pocket by $10,000—so you just let it go, and your only loss is the $500 premium (as it's called). You could alternatively have bought the right to sell the Ferrari for $50,000—in which case your preferences would be reversed, and you'd be hoping that the price had dropped. In that event you'd buy the car for $40,000 and immediately sell it for $10,000 more. Futures are the same as options, except that they bring with them the obligation to buy or sell at the specified price: with a future, you are committed to the deal. It follows that futures are much riskier than options.

Options and futures have been very important products in the history of finance, and it is no coincidence that these derivatives were first extensively developed in commodities markets, especially the Chicago Mercantile Exchange (which started life 110 years ago as the Chicago Butter and Egg Board). For years, derivatives existed as useful tools of this type. They were immensely practical but not in their basic essence too complicated. They've been around for a long time: speculation on tulip derivatives was a feature of the Dutch tulip bubble in 1637. Their use has long been widespread, and their history involves some entertaining byways, for instance the fact that the U.S. Confederacy funded its war against the Union with a derivative bond to attract foreign currency.

As soon as the market in derivatives was professionalized at the Chicago exchange, it quickly became obvious that there was a huge potential market in the field of financial derivatives, which derived their value not from eggs or butter or wheat but from shares. The market, however, was hampered by one big thing: no one could work out how to price the derivatives. The interacting factors of time, risk, interest rates, and price volatility were so complex that they defeated mathematicians until Fischer Black and Myron

Scholes published their paper in 1973, one month after the
Chicago Board Options Exchange had opened for business.
[The revolutionary aspect of Black and Scholes's paper was
an equation enabling people to calculate the price of financial derivatives based on the value of the underlying assets.]
The Black-Scholes formula opened up a whole new area of
derivatives trading. It was a defining moment in the mathe-
matization of the market. Within months, traders were using equations and vocabulary straight out of Black-Scholes
(as it is now universally known) and the worldwide derivatives business took off like a rocket. The total market in derivative products around the world is today counted in the
hundreds of trillions of dollars. Nobody knows the exact
figure, but the notional amount certainly exceeds the total
value of all the world's economic output, roughly $66 tril-
lion, by a huge factor—perhaps tenfold. This apparently
impossible fact is explained by the difference between the
underlying value of the products and the notional values
wrapped up in derivatives deriving from them. Say you're a
pig farmer and you want to sell your next season's pork
bellies in advance, to lock in a good price. A trader buys
the bellies for $100,000, and your part in the story of the
pork bellies is done; but that doesn't mean the contract to
deliver the bellies has finished its adventures in the financial
system. The trader sells it to another trader, who sells it to
a third dealer, who's worried that he overpaid on some bellies earlier in the year and now wants to reduce the average
price paid, but the person to whom he sells the contract
holds on to it for a bit and then sells it on, because the price
for next-season pork bellies in general is rising and your
belly contract—which is what is being traded here, a pork
belly derivative contract—has gone up in value. So now the
real value of the bellies has stayed at the $100,000 for

which you sold it, whereas the derivatives have now been traded four times, to create $400,000 of notional action. Hence the term "notional"—these aren't really deals for the bellies but for the derivative of the bellies, the contract to deliver them; hence also the way in which the value of notional contracts can spiral far, far away from the underlying real assets.*

Even once it's been explained, however, it still seems wholly contrary to common sense that the market for products that derive from real things should be unimaginably vaster than the market for the things themselves. With derivatives, we seem to enter a modernist world in which risk no longer means what it means in plain English and in which there is a profound break between the language of finance and that of common sense. It is difficult for civilians to understand a derivatives contract or any of the range of closely related instruments. These are all products that were designed initially to transfer or hedge risks—to purchase some insurance against the prospect of a price going down, when your main bet was that the price would go up. The farmer selling his next season's crop might not have understood a modern financial derivative, but he would have recognized that use of it.

In an ideal world, one populated by vegetarians, Esperanto speakers, and fluffy bunny wabbits, derivatives would be used for one thing only: to reduce risk. Because they are

---

* With all that trading at a remove from the real asset, it's tempting to wonder if people ever forget they've bought a derivatives contract and end up with a huge quantity of pork bellies or coffee being dumped on their doorstep six months after doing a derivatives deal. There is a perhaps apocryphal story that John Maynard Keynes, when bursar of King's College Cambridge, once forgot he'd made a bet on wheat futures and had to accept delivery of several tons of wheat, which he then had stored in the college cellars.

bought "on margin"—that is, not for the full cost of the underlying asset but for the advance premium, as in the hypothetical Ferrari example above—they offer a cheap and flexible form of insurance against things going wrong. Imagine, for instance, that you are convinced that the stock market will go up by 50 percent in the next year. You know it in your waters—so much so that you borrow $100,000 and use it to buy shares. If the market goes up, you'll be pleased with yourself; but if you're wrong and the market plunges, you'll be badly out of pocket—unless you take out some insurance. So you buy a $10,000 option to sell shares at a lower price than you paid for them. That money is wasted if your shares go up—but you won't care much because your main position is in serious profit. But if shares go down, you have some insurance—you can cash in the option to sell shares at the lower price and eliminate most of your losses. This is called "hedging": you have used an option to hedge your main risk.

Alas, we don't live in that kinder, gentler world. In reality, the power of derivatives has a way of proving irresistible for people who aren't just sure that the market is going up but who are beyond sure, are supersure, are possessed of absolute knowledge. Financial experts are often possessed of this kind of certainty. In that event, it's very tempting indeed to buy an option that increases your level of risk, in the knowledge that this will increase your level of reward. In the above example, instead of hedging the position with an option to sell, you could magnify it with options to buy, which will be worth a lot if you're right—sorry, *when* you're right. When you're right and the market goes up by half, your $10,000 option will be worth $50,000 (that's the $50,000 by which the shares have gone up). In fact, instead of buying $100,000 of shares and a $10,000 option to buy, why not instead buy $100,000 worth of options? This is called leverage: you have leveraged your $100,000 to buy $1,000,000 worth of exposure to the market. That way, when you get your price rise, you will have made $500,000, and all with borrowed money. In fact, since you're not just confident but certain, why not skip the option and instead buy some futures, which are cheaper (because riskier)—let's say half the price? These futures, at $5,000 each, oblige you to buy twenty lots of the shares for $100,000 each in a year's time. Hooray! You're rich! Unless the market, instead of doubling, halves, and you are saddled with an obligation to buy $2 million worth of shares which are now worth only $1 million. You've just borrowed $100,000 and through the power of modern financial instruments used it to lose $1 million. Whoops.

It might seem unlikely that anyone would do anything that stupid, but in practice it happens all the time. The list of individual traders who have lost more than a billion dollars at a time betting on derivatives is not short: Robert Citron of Orange County, California; Toshihide Iguchi at Daiwa Bank; Yasuo Hamanaka at Sumitomo Corporation; Nick Leeson of Barings Bank; and now, most recently and spectacularly of all, Jérôme Kerviel of Société Générale. These are the traders who have each single-handedly managed to lose more than a billion dollars of their employers' money. Hamanaka used to be the poster boy—he lost $2.6 billion betting on copper in 1996. But Kerviel's $7.2 billion loss betting on European stock markets made that figure look a little dated and nineties, especially since, according to his bank, he began accumulating the losses the same month he was caught. ¡Olé! In Leeson's case, it was a huge unauthorized position in futures on the Nikkei 225 (the main Japanese stock exchange) which destroyed Barings in

1995. Leeson had been doubling and redoubling his bets in the belief/hope that the index would rise and hiding the resulting open position—a gigantic open-ended bet—in a secret account. (Incidentally, Leeson's big bet was on the Nikkei holding its level above 19,000. At the time of writing, fourteen years later, the index sits at 9,287—proof, if it were needed, that when prices go down they can stay that way for a long time.) The loss eventually amounted to £880 million, and destroyed Barings, Britain's oldest merchant bank. The year before it went broke, the chairman of the company, Peter Baring, urbanely told the governor of the Bank of England that "it is not actually all that difficult to make money in the securities business."

The power of derivatives is one of the main things about them—their ability to hedge risk, but also, and much more alarmingly, to magnify it. The second main thing about them is their complexity. We are a long, long way from a single quote for next season's wheat crop. The contemporary derivative is likely to involve a mix of options, futures, currencies, and debt, structured and priced in ways which are the closest extant thing to rocket science. Mathematics Ph.D.s are all over the place in this business. Some of the derivatives involved are actively designed to conceal the real nature of the assets—bearing in mind that the assets involved are themselves often debts, repackaged and sold on in "black box" structures designed to hide the entities within. The products thus created are way over the heads of civilians and sometimes, it seems, over the heads of most of the people who buy and sell them. "We invented this stuff, so we know how it works," my friend Tony told me, referring to the fact that his bank was one of the first players in the derivatives market. "But I get the feeling that a lot of the banks are doing it just because other people are doing it—they don't really know what they're doing."

This is one point at which we have to face one of the central facts of modern banking, the way it has been taken over by advanced mathematics. 'Twas not ever thus. My father, as I've already said, worked for a bank. He arrived in London for the first time in 1948 with a degree from the University of Melbourne and, thanks to his time in the Australian army, fluent Japanese. As a result he ended up getting a job with the Hongkong and Shanghai Bank and spending almost all his working life in Asia. The bank he worked for was then a conservative institution, heavily watermarked with its colonial origins but also a well-run company which was beginning to grow: it's now a global giant, the twenty-first biggest company in the world. In 1948, it was a fairly typical bank in many respects, including the following: in my father's generation of newly hired managers, he was the only person with a degree. The fact that he had been to university made him stand out as a semi-intellectual. Half a century later, HSBC liked to hire only people with first-class degrees from Oxbridge, and preferably in mathematics and the physical sciences. That's one effect of the mathematicization of banking, which hit hard and apparently irrevocably in the 1990s, as bankers began to use new tools and techniques derived from supercomplex math. In his brilliant book about risk, *Fooled by Randomnesss: The Hidden Role of Chance in Life and the Markets,* Nassim Taleb describes those as the days when "every plane from Moscow had at least its back row full of Russian mathematical physicists en route to Wall Street." One of the consequences of this new turn in banking was that there could be significant gaps inside banks between the senior managers and the "quants," as the mathemati-

cians are called. (A friend of mine who did an MBA at Stan-
ford told me that on his course, students had to identify
themselves as being either "quants" or "poets.") The managers liked what the quants could do, but they didn't always understand it—with consequences which now, alas,
are becoming clear. A very senior Treasury figure reports
that a bank board member came up to him at a social function and said he had some good news: "We're no longer
going to get involved in things we don't understand." He
added, "We now own his bank."

Derivatives are a central part of this new mathematical
complexity. One of their main uses is in arbitrage. That's
the name of investments which effectively bet both ways on
the market, exploiting small differences in price to make
what should be risk-free profits. (It's what Nick Leeson was
supposed to be doing, exploiting tiny differences in the
price of Nikkei 225 futures between the Osaka exchange,
where trading was electronic, and the Singapore exchange,
where it wasn't. The gap in price would last only for a couple of seconds, and in that gap Barings would buy low and
sell high—a guaranteed, risk-free profit.) The complexity of
the mathematics involved in derivatives can't be exagger-
ated. This was the reason John Meriwether, a famous bond
trader, employed Myron Scholes—he of the Black-Scholes
equation—and Robert Merton, the man with whom he
shared the 1997 Nobel Prize in Economics, to be directors
and cofounders of his new hedge fund, Long-Term Capital
Management.* The idea was to use these big brains to cre-

* I don't talk much about hedge funds because they don't feature centrally
in the story of the credit crunch. The main question people ask about
hedge funds is a simple one: what are they? And the simple answer is, they
are largely unregulated pools of investment capital. The whole point of
them is to evade the rules around other sorts of publicly traded pooled

ate a highly leveraged, arbitraged, no-risk investment portfolio designed to profit no matter what happened, whether
the market went up, down, or sideways or popped out for
a cheese sandwich. LTCM quadrupled in value in its first
four years, then imploded in the chaos that followed
Russia's default on its foreign-debt obligations in 1998.
The fund had equity of $4.72 billion, which would have
been pretty healthy if it were not for the fact that it was exposed, thanks to the miracles of borrowing, leverage, and
derivatives, to $1.25 trillion of risk. So if it went broke,
LTCM would leave a $1.25 trillion hole in the global finan-
cial system. The big brains had made a classic mistake:
they treated a very unlikely thing (the default and its consequences) as if it were impossible. As Keynes—he who
made himself and his college rich by spending half an hour
a day in bed playing the stock market—once observed,
there is nothing so disastrous as a rational policy in an irrational world. Keynes was preoccupied by the difference between risk in the sense of the mathematical calculation of
probabilities—which is what we're discussing here—and
uncertainty, the more profound unknowabilities of life and
history. You can manage risk, in the sense that you can calculate probabilities and allow for them, but you can't really
manage uncertainty, not in that precisely calculable way.
Confuse risk with uncertainty, and you have dug a tank
trap for yourself. That's what happened with LTCM. It was
caught in the gap between mathematically assessible risks,

---

capital such as investment trusts. The name is misleading, verging on useless. It refers to the idea that some funds "hedge" their investments and
aim to create structures which make money irrespective of whether the
market goes up or down, and with lower levels of risk than the stock market. This is often done using large amounts of borrowed money, our old
buddy leverage.

such as those embodied in its beautiful models, and a nasty
piece of real-world uncertainty, which took the form—as
uncertainty tends to do—of something nobody expected:
the Russian default.

It couldn't have happened without derivatives, which in
their modern form are the most powerful and most complicated financial instruments ever devised. And they are everywhere. More than $1 trillion worth of derivatives are
bought and sold every day, many of them in London. Every
single thing which can be traded through derivatives is. In
the words of Warren Buffett, the greatest living stock market investor, "The range of derivatives contracts is limited
only by the imagination of man (or sometimes, so it seems,
madmen). At Enron, for example, newsprint and broad-
band derivatives, due to be settled many years in the future,
were put on the books. Or say you want to write a contract
speculating on the number of twins to be born in Nebraska
in 2020. No problem—at a price, you will easily find an
obliging counterparty." 2 Many companies which look as if
their business is to do other things are in reality in the derivatives business, Enron being the best-known example.
Buffett is a derivativephobe, not least because he prefers to
know what's going on in the companies he invests in, and
derivatives make that effectively impossible. He also, with
a prescience so pure it verges on the spooky, said in 2002:[3]

> The derivatives genie is now well out of the bottle,
> and these instruments will almost certainly multiply
> in variety and number until some event makes their
> toxicity clear. Knowledge of how dangerous they are
> has already permeated the electricity and gas busi-
> nesses, in which the eruption of major troubles
> caused the use of derivatives to diminish dramati-

cally. Elsewhere, however, the derivatives business continues to expand unchecked. Central banks and governments have so far found no effective way to control, or even monitor, the risks posed by these contracts.

Buffett was horribly right about the risks. The irony is that he wasn't even talking here about the category of derivative which turned out to be the most destructive of all, the credit default swap, or CDS. I am going to arraign a number of culprits for the crash: derivatives are one of the main ones, but among derivatives, it was CDS which were the chief baddy, the gang leader, the Mafia don, the most destructive of the WMDs. As with some other culprits in the crisis, credit default swaps were a new thing, invented by bankers seeking newer, sexier ways of making newer, sexier profits.

When I first began to study the world of the City, I found it hard to come to grips with the idea that financial instruments are "invented," cooked up in the same way as works of art or scientific theories—but the fact is that they are. Credit default swaps are complicated, but they're based on an old idea, that of a more straightforward kind of swap. Say you're in the grocery business and feel gloomy about its prospects. Your immediate neighbor is in the stationery business, and he feels gloomy about his prospects but less so about yours. You fall to discussing this, and one of you hits on a brilliant idea: why not just swap revenues? You take his profits for the year, and he takes yours. You continue to do what you're doing, and so does he—but you agree to swap your financial assets. The actual business doesn't change hands, thus making the swap, in banking terminology, "synthetic." Another example: Your mortgage has five years to run and is at a fixed rate, and you're deeply pissed off about that, because you think interest rates are going to fall and you are paying more than you should. You fall to moaning about this with your next-door neighbor, but instead of commiserating he starts to sing the blues about his own variable-rate mortgage, which he is certain is about to get more expensive, because he disagrees with you and thinks interest rates are about to go up. Aha! The two of you have a Eureka! moment. Why don't you just swap and pay each other's mortgages? That way you can take the position you want to on interest rates without having to do anything complicated like selling your house or remortgaging. Again, this is a "synthetic" deal, because the underlying assets—the houses—haven't changed hands.

Swaps first arrived in the corporate world in 1981. The first of them featured IBM exchanging surplus Swiss francs and deutsche marks for dollars held by the World Bank: the two institutions exchanged their bond earnings and their obligations to bondholders without actually exchanging the bonds. They needed to hedge their currency risks and increase their holdings in other currencies, and they chose to do so through a swap rather than going through the expense, and the risk, of issuing new bond instruments or making new currency investments of their own.

A word here about bonds. In business, companies regularly need to raise money—to raise capital. They need to build new factories, expand into new markets, make a big push on advertising spending, take over a competitor, or whatever: for some reason or another, they need to raise money. There are three primary ways of doing that. The first is to borrow from a bank. The second is to sell some of their equity—in plain English, to sell shares—as in the example in the previous chapter, where You Inc. sells a

10 percent share of itself. This can be hard, psychologically, to get used to. In fact, one of my former employers, Conrad Black, the onetime proprietor of the Telegraph newspapers, is currently in prison in Florida, apparently for failing to grasp this point. He took his company, Hollinger, public and then complained about the fuss and bother that his new shareholders made, saying that they had failed to understand that the whole point of going public was that it enabled him to make "relatively cheap use of other people's capital." Black was subsequently tried on charges of taking that idea a little too literally. But in any case, just from a theoretical and ideological point of view, he was completely wrong. People who own your business's equity own your business and are not in general inclined to forget the fact.

That's one of several reasons why companies that need capital often prefer to go down the third route for raising money. That is to sell bonds: in other words, to borrow money from the markets. Debt is therefore a fundamental fact of how capital works, and it's important to understand that a lot of the time, in the corporate world, debt is a good thing. This is one way in which examples from personal finances—where, if we're sensible, we try to avoid debt—are misleading. In business, debt is a useful, even an indispensable, tool. Example: You have a business making cakes. You invest $100,000 in your own business and it makes a profit of 10 percent, so at the end of the year you are $10,000 ahead, meaning you've put your capital to work and it's earned you a return of 10 percent: not bad. But see what happens if you decide to expand your business by borrowing money. You go to the bank and get a loan of $200,000 to invest in your business, at an interest rate of 4 percent. You now make $300,000 worth of cake. Given that you're still making 10 percent, that's $30,000 gross profit. You pay your 4 percent to the bank at a cost of $8,000, and look what's happened: by borrowing money, you increased your profit from $10,000 to $22,000, a 120 percent increase, achieved through the benign miracle of debt. This is sometimes called "leverage," confusingly since the same name is given to the difference between equity and liabilities described in the previous chapter; but the underlying idea is similar, that of using other people's money to make your own money work harder.

During the credit bubble, levels of this sort of leverage reached astonishing proportions. The extent and importance of debt and leverage are two of the things which seem natural to financial insiders but are hard for civilians to fully grasp. Talking to insiders about debt can make you feel like a bit of a country mouse. Chatting with Tony one day, I wondered aloud why a particular entrepreneur had gone into the restaurant and club business, which isn't famous for generating huge profits. His reply was instant: "It'll have a good cash stream, and he'll just leverage it up. Say he's losing a million a year but has ten million in cash coming it. He leverages it twenty times, suddenly he's got two hundred million to play with, and the million quid a year he's losing is nothing." Don't try this at home . . . well, I say that, but in fact, home may be exactly where you are trying it. The commonest form of large-scale leverage in most people's lives is the mortgage: you leverage your income by a factor of three or four to make a single big long-term, highly illiquid investment, in the form of a property. There seems to be something of a conspiracy to discourage us from thinking of mortgages quite as baldly and bluntly as that. Ads for share investments are obliged to warn people that values can go down as well as up, but there's no such reminder about our biggest and least liquid investments of all. Instead, the reminders come in the form of brutal reality checks, such as the current downturn in housing prices.

Government debt is different from business debt and instead is a little more like personal debt—which basically involves borrowing from your future earnings in order to spend money in the present day. In order to do that, governments issue bonds, in the same way that companies do. The British government is selling £225 billion of these bonds this year, to raise the money it needs to pay for all its spending. These numbers are scarily big, but then the whole bond market is scarily big. This is a huge, huge part of the global economy, absolutely central to its functioning. Although the stock market gets more attention and has more name recognition among the general public, bonds are arguably even more important to the operation of the money world. It adds up to a lot of money: the total value of the global bond market is in the region of $50 trillion. Bonds are, for governments and for many corporations, the single most fundamental way of raising money. A bond repays an agreed rate of interest until it matures, and all of these things are fixed: the price of the bond, the rate of interest it pays, and the date when it matures. In the case of You Ltd., you might raise the $10,000 you need by selling a bond for $10,000 which will pay, say, 5 percent interest every year for five years—that's $500 a year. At the end of that time, you promise to buy back the bond for its face value, $10,000.

Is that a good deal? Maybe yes, maybe no. It depends on a lot of things, such as how likely you are to be able to keep up the payments—so if you seem like a bad risk, you'll have to pay more interest for the money you want to borrow. The safety, or nonsafety, of your debt is rated by a number of agencies, which have a hugely important role in the running of the credit markets. The best known of these agencies are Moody's Investors Service and Standard & Poor's—names which, it has to be admitted, have a slightly ironic edge in current times, given how badly some of their debt ratings have malfunctioned and given also that "moody" is a synonym for, in the words of Jonathon Green's great *Cassell's Dictionary of Slang*, "illicit, uncertain, false." The highest-rated debt in the world is AAA, the same status as U.S. government Treasury bills; the ratings thereafter go down through AA and then A down through BBB, BB, B, CCC, and then R, which means the cops have been called.* Any debt of BBB and above is known as "investment grade"; any below BBB is known as a "junk bond" on the basis that its level of risk is high— but that shouldn't make it sound as if junk bonds are a marginal or unrespectable form of finance. (You may well feel that the distinction between investment and speculation is a little blurry and subjective, and you would be right. There is a character in one of Anthony Powell's early novels, a retired major gone stone broke and living in a boardinghouse owing to "having squandered all his money in judicious investments.") Because they have to pay high rates of interest, junk bonds can be very useful for investors; if they didn't exist, only supersafe companies would be able to raise money, and all sorts of inventions and investments and growth would be impossible. The important thing is that all those involved should be well aware of what they're getting into.

If You Inc.'s bond is given a high rating by the agencies,

---

*The two companies use slightly different lettering systems; this is the S&P version.

it can pay a lower rate of interest—its debt is safer and therefore pays less well. If it's given a lower rating, it will have to pay out more. In time, as interest rates in the wider economy go up and down, the You Inc. five-year bond will be more or less attractive to investors. If interest rates drop to 2 percent, that 5 percent will suddenly look tasty, and the person who bought the bond might well be tempted to sell it on at a profit to someone else in need of a nice earner; conversely, if interest rates zoom up and it's easy to get a 7 percent interest rate, the 5 percent will look less appealing, and the price of the You Inc. bond will drop. It will also drop as the bond comes closer to maturity. This is the point when You Inc. will buy it back in return for the cash value stated on the bond; obviously, the closer in time the bond is to the point when it will be worth exactly $10,000, the more the price will converge on that figure. All these factors coincide to make the global bond market a huge, complicated, multiply overlapping and profoundly interwoven thing, with a colossal number of working parts and therefore immense opportunities for swapping and trading and exchanging of revenue streams.

This is where, in 1981, swaps entered into the story.[4] Swaps began life as a way of exchanging revenue between different types of bonds. The first deal, brokered by Salomon Brothers, was worth $210 million for ten years and kick-started a whole new field of finance. Companies would swap bonds and equivalent products, and in this way gain access to one other's lines of business: it was a way for firms to spread their economic tentacles while not actually diverging from their own core business. In particular, swaps took off as a way of playing around with other firms' interest rates and exposure to different currencies. By the summer of 1994, swaps had become a roaringly successful feature of the banking world: the volume of interest rate and currency derivatives traded was $12 trillion, more than was generated by the entire U.S. economy.

One of the main players in this market was the bank J.P. Morgan. Banks have different characters, based on their different histories and institutional personalities; this is true not just of banks but of most companies and indeed most institutions. The bank J.P. Morgan is named after its founder, John Pierpont Morgan, a financier of legendary power, wealth, and status and an extraordinary collector of art. In the world of money, Morgan is famous for having rescued the entire U.S. banking system from collapse not once but twice, during the panics of 1893 (when he directly lent the U.S. Treasury millions of dollars to buy gold) and 1907 (when he held a vital series of meetings with senior bankers at his house and bullied them into joint action to keep the system solvent). This amount of power, and his considerable physical presence, combined to give him a sinister aura, magnificently captured in E. L. Doctorow's novel *Ragtime,* in which the financier's interest in occult practices and secret knowledge causes him to spend a night in the innermost chamber of the Great Pyramid, in the pursuit of who knows what secret wisdom—which makes it odder that in photographs he looks chubby and bland, an unpenetrating walrus of a man with a bulbous nose and heroic mustache.

The bank J.P. Morgan was more like the man's photograph than his reputation: it was a superrespectable old-school Wall Street firm with a long list of similarly respectable clients. It was also one of two firms to carry on J.P.'s legacy: the other was the financial services company Morgan Stanley. The first incarnation of J.P. Morgan was broken into two in 1933 by the Glass-Steagall Act, passed during the Great Depression, which forced retail banks, that is, the ordinary sort of banks with which we're all familiar, to split from investment banks, the sort which issue complex financial instruments, trade on capital markets, and run mergers and acquisitions. I call the two types the piggy bank and the casino; the idea behind Glass-Steagall was that the casino activities shouldn't be allowed to endanger the banks which look after the deposits of the general public.

By the 1990s, J.P. Morgan was deeply involved in the swaps market. That market had boomed since the IBM–World Bank swap; the trouble was that it had boomed too much. Everyone was now executing swaps, which was driving down profit margins and making them less profitable. So in 1994, the J.P. Morgan swaps team went on an off-site weekend to Boca Raton, Florida, to come up with a new, and therefore newly lucrative, product to sell. Now, the world of banking operates according to different norms from the rest of the corporate and business world. The off-site corporate weekend is one example. Normal behavior on these occasions consists of punishing the minibar and nursing consequent hangovers, hitting on long-fancied colleagues, and putting embarrassing items, ideally pornographic films, on one another's hotel bills. For form's sake, a few new ideas are cooked up and then gradually allowed to die a natural death when everyone is back at work and liver function levels have returned to normal. Bankers, however, are different. On their off-site weekend, J.P. Morgan's team confirmed to normative behavior in certain respects. Binge drinking occurred; a senior colleague's nose was broken; a trashed jet ski and many cheeseburgers were charged to somebody else's account. It has always been thus. Where the J.P. Morgan team broke with tradition was in the fact that it also came up with a real idea—an idea which turned out not only to be huge but to change the entire nature of modern banking, with consequences that are currently rocking the economy of the entire planet.

The idea that the J.P. Morgan team had was for an innovative kind of swap. Translated into the terms of personal finance, this is how it worked. Say your neighbors the Smiths approach you and ask to borrow some money—say, to pay for a loft conversion. You happen to have a spare $100,000 in cash, which is the amount they want to borrow, and they promise to pay you a good rate of interest, say $1,000 a month (just to keep the numbers simple) and then to pay back the principal at the end of the year. So you make the loan, and then you fall to wondering what happens if the Smiths can't make their loan payments, on which you are relying for handy extra income. At which point you ask your other neighbors, the Joneses, if they are interested in making a little bit of cash on the side. They say yes, and so you swap with them: they take on the risk that the Smiths won't pay the loan—in other words, if the Smiths default, the Joneses will make up the money—and in return you pay them a fee, say, $50 a month. In effect, what you've done is taken out a form of insurance. So the Smiths get their $100,000; you get your $1,000 a month; the Joneses get their $50 a month. If the Smiths stop being able to pay you, you collect from the Joneses instead.

Notice that there is one huge benefit from this deal: you have managed to lend money, at a good rate of interest, at *no risk*. You've insured the risk away. It's a basic law of money that risk is correlated to reward—the amount of money you can make is determined by the amount of risk you are willing to take on. But you've just engineered the risk out of existence. If the Smiths stop being able to pay you, you collect the money from the Joneses instead. That, when you fall to thinking about it, opens up all sorts of potential . . .

———————

This, translated into the corporate world of bonds and loans, was the new idea: to swap the risk of default. In effect, it was to sell the risk that a borrower wouldn't be able to pay back a debt. This had enormous potential in the world of banking. Since banking is based on making loans to customers, the risk of default by those customers is a hugely important part of the business. So a product which made it possible to reduce that risk—to reduce it by selling it to somebody else—had the potential to create a gigantic new market. The new idea was a product which would resemble a kind of insurance, with the product insured being the risk of default on a specific debt. The first such deal involved the oil company Exxon, which needed to open a line of credit to cover potential damages of $5 billion resulting from the oil spillage from the *Exxon Valdez* in 1989. Exxon was an old client of J.P. Morgan, which was therefore reluctant to turn them down, even though the deal would take up a lot of capital which the bank could use more profitably elsewhere. Banks had rules about the amount of capital they needed to keep against the eventuality of loans going bad. The Basel rules, named after the city in Switzerland where they were formulated, are the internationally accepted code of practice for banking. These rules required that banks hold 8 percent of their capital in reserve against the risk of outstanding loans. For the bankers, that was a drag. It limited the amount of lending they could make, the amount of risk they could take on, and therefore the level of profit they could achieve. If they lent the money to Exxon, they would have to keep an amount equivalent to

8 percent of it in reserve, just sitting there, instead of going out into the markets and making more money.

At which thought, a lightbulb went on. Blythe Masters, one of the Boca Raton swaps team, came up with the idea of selling the credit line to the European Bank for Reconstruction and Development, in return for a fee. So if Exxon asked for the money, the EBRD would cough it up—and in return, it would pocket a fee from J.P. Morgan for taking on the risk. Exxon would get its credit line, J.P. Morgan would get to honor its client relationship but also to keep its capital reserves intact for sexier activities, and EBRD would get the fees. The deal was so new it didn't even have a name: eventually the one settled on was "credit default swap." If the risk of loans could be sold, however, it logically followed that loans were now risk-free; and if that was the case, surely it made sense that the capital involved—since it wasn't at risk—was free to be re-lent, without counting against the reserve requirements of the Basel rules. No harm, no foul; no risk, no need to suck up useful capital. After months of work and haggling about the rules, the deal was allowed by the regulators, who accepted the idea that the selling of risk in this way was a good thing, because it spread that risk out through the financial system rather than concentrating it in one place.

So far, so good for J.P. Morgan. But the deal had been laborious and time-consuming, and the bank wouldn't be able to make real money out of credit default swaps until the process became streamlined and industrialized. In the above personal finance example, the personal nature of the deal is part of the point: you know your neighbors and can make a decision about how likely they are to pay you back and therefore how safe your investment is. To make real money out of these deals, however, it would be so much more lucrative if one could just skip past that stage—if there were a way of bypassing all the tedious, case-by-case, look-them-in-the-eye stage of assessing the risk of default.

The invention which allowed all this to happen was securitization. The issue with credit default swaps was the underlying issue with all banking, everywhere and always: the risk that the person to whom you're lending money won't be able to pay you back. Every loan is a specific case which needs assessing on its merits, and it's hard to industrialize the process of deciding case by case. The EBRD-Exxon deal, for instance, took months of intense work to arrange (and the first commercial swap, the IBM–World Bank arrangement, had taken a full two years). What securitization did was bundle together a package of such loans and then rely on safety in numbers and the law of averages: even if some loans did default, the others wouldn't; they would keep the stream of revenue going, and thus the risk of default would be spread and minimized. So there would be two sources of revenue, as well as of fees: one from the sale of the loans and another from the steady flow of repayments. And then someone had another idea: that the securities could be divided up into different levels of risk and sold off accordingly, into riskier and less risky "tranches" of debt, all paying different rates of interest in return for differing levels of risk. Some customers would want the high-paying debt, which, it went without saying, was higher risk; others would like the safer but less lucrative flavor. Customers would be able to buy exactly the degree of risk they wanted, tailor-made to their needs. All these ideas were knocking around the banking world. William Demchak at J.P. Morgan put them together to create securitized bundles of credit default swaps—bundles of insurance against default—and selling them to investors. The investors would get the streams of revenue, according to the level of risk and reward they chose; the bank would get insurance against its loans and fees for setting up the deal.

There was one final component of the J.P. Morgan team's invention. It set up an offshore shell company, called a special purpose vehicle, or SPV, to fulfill the role supplied by the EBRD in the first credit default swap. The shell company would assume $9.7 billion of J.P. Morgan's risk; then it would sell off that risk to investors in the form of securities paying differing rates of interest. So the risk of default was sold to the SPV, then pooled, made into a range of securities, and sold on to investors. Why do banks bother to set up SPVs? Two reasons. The first was to remove the swap from the bank's balance sheet. The more assets banks have on their balance sheet, in proportion to their equity, the more leveraged they are: if the assets didn't appear on the balance sheet, the bank would look less leveraged and therefore safer. What regulators and investors didn't know couldn't hurt them. In addition, the SPVs were located offshore, in places such as the Caymans, Bermuda, the Bahamas, or the British Virgin Islands, for the simple reason of avoiding taxes. In this case, the really beautiful part was that according to J.P. Morgan's calculations, the underlying loans were so safe that it needed to sell only $700 million of insurance to cover $9.7 billion of debt. The credit agency Moody's hummed and hawed for a while before agreeing, and behold: a whole new era in banking had dawned. J.P. Morgan had found a way to shift risk off its books, while simultaneously generating income from that risk and freeing up capital to lend elsewhere. It was magic. The only thing wrong with it was the name, BISTRO—standing for Broad Index Secured Trust Offering but making the new rocket-science financial instrument sound like a place you went to for a plate of steak frites. The market came to prefer a different term: "synthetic collateralized debt obligations."

Just to keep track of where we have got to with these new financial instruments, let's translate it back into personal finance terms. Remember your arrangement to lend money to the Smiths for their loft—the one you got your other neighbors, the Joneses, to insure. That was a straightforward swap of risk. The deal went fine, and you fell to thinking about how it might be improved if another neighbor were to approach you. You've started to be a little bit annoyed by the way in which that loan tied up the full $100,000 of spare capital that you had at your disposal. When another neighbor, the Wilsons, hear that you lent the Smiths money and ask you to make them a similar loan, you're in a position to come up with something a little bit more creative. For one thing, you know that the money you're lending is totally safe. Because the Smiths are doing up their house, the capital you've lent is adding to the value of their house, which means that in your view it's not at risk. So what you do now is re-lend your $100,000 to the Wilsons. As for where do you get the money from—does it matter, since you're on to a surefire winner? House prices are zooming up in your area, so there's nothing to worry about from the capital point of view. The $100,000 simply isn't at risk. What's the worst that could happen? The Smiths or Wilsons might have a cash crisis and, okay, say it all goes wrong and they can't pay you back and eventually have to sell their house. You'll definitely get back your $100,000, so the only thing you're at risk of losing is the $12,000 of interest they owe you—and you sell that risk to the Joneses again, so again you've engineered away the risk. But wait! Now another neighbor, the Millers, approach, also wanting to do the same sort of deal. They're up for it,

you're up for it, the Joneses are up for it, the only trouble is
that you've run out of capital because you've already lent
your $100,000 twice, to the Smiths and the Wilsons. But
since that money is in your view completely safe, you
should feel free to lend it again. So what you do is create a
company, ideally based offshore, where it pays no U.K. tax,
and extend to it the credit to buy the loan from you. You
lend it a virtual $100,000, it buys the Wilsons' debt from
you and recredits you with the $100,000, so you're back in
the black. (In practice, the personal finance example breaks
down here, because you can't lend money to yourself and
create credit in quite this way. But large financial institutions can and do.) Now your company, Lofts Inc., sells the
default risk on the Wilsons' debt—the credit default swap—
to the Joneses. And then when another neighbor comes to
you and again asks to borrow your $100,000, you do the
same thing, and then again, and again, up to, let's say for
the sake of this example, ten times. The cash is pouring in,
and everybody wins: the neighbors get their loft money,
you get your stream of repayment fees paid to your offshore company, the Joneses get their stream of insurance
payments, and the beauty of it is that there's no risk for
you, because you've insured it away. You can stop car-
ing about whether or not your neighbors actually can pay
you back. If they can't, so what? The Joneses will pick up
the tab.

The beauties of this, from a financial engineering point
of view, are almost too numerous. The new CDS instruments are a magnificently efficient way of spreading, and
therefore minimizing, risk—at least they are if used as their
initial inventors intended. Financial crashes and implosions
are often linked to overconcentration of risk: placing too
big bets in one place. At the time of the invention of the

CDS, the most recent large-scale bust in the United States was the savings and loan debacle of the 1980s, in which overconcentration of risk on the part of the savings and loans played a prominent role. One of the reasons why regulators were minded to look favorably on CDSs was that they saw them as useful devices for dispersing and therefore diminishing risk. No one foresaw the possibility that they might spread unmanageable and nearly undetectable amounts of risk throughout the financial system. A second attractive aspect: the new instruments offered a whole new way of participating in somebody else's business. Remember that there are two basic ways of investing in companies, which are also the two basic ways for companies to raise capital: stocks, in which you buy a piece of a company, and bonds, in which you lend the company money. The genius thing about CDSs was that they offered a third way. You got a string of regular payments (as with a bond), and you exposed yourself to the risk of the other party defaulting (as in a bond), but it was sexier than a bond, because your capital wasn't fully tied up in the process. You didn't need to draw on it unless the counterparty defaulted. Add a bit of financial ingenuity, and you could use your capital very effectively over and over again, because you needed to post only part of the capital as collateral against the risk of default. In terms of the above example, say the Joneses were covering $100,000 of risk; the rules might dictate that they needed to have only $10,000 on hand against that. If they were sitting on $100,000 of cash, they could guarantee up to ten times that amount of risk, so their $100,000 would earn them $1,000,000 of CDS business. That's sexy indeed. So the miracle of credit default swaps has enabled you to take $100,000 and lend it ten times, and then sell the CDS ten times to other people who have $100,000 to risk. The CDS has done an amazing job of putting your capital to work.

These new financial instruments were very, very clever, but they had an unfortunate side effect: they broke banking. They did so because banking at its heart is, or should be, a simple business. Customers deposit money in a bank in return for interest; the bank lends that money to other people at a higher rate of interest. This isn't glamorous or interesting, but then banking is not supposed to resemble base jumping or hip-hop. Instead it is a guaranteed way of making steady money forever (and not incidentally of creating credit in the economy), as long as one all-important rule is followed: the bank has to be careful about to whom it lends money. The quality of the loans it makes is crucial, because those loans are the bank's earning assets. This isn't some incidental or marginal issue, it's the very core of what banking is. The trouble with the model of packaging plus securitization was that it broke with the fundamental principle that a bank had to individually assess and monitor every loan. The new instruments made that impossible. The mathematics of valuation models—horrendously complex equations to assess probabilities and correlations, cooked up in the best mad-scientist style by the firms' math "quants"—took the burden of assessing statistical risk. The whole idea that a banker looks a borrower in the eye and makes a decision on whether he can trust him came to seem laughably nineteenth century. As for the risks, well, as Lawrence Summers said when he was deputy secretary of the Treasury, "the parties to these kinds of contract are largely sophisticated financial institutions that would appear to be eminently capable of protecting themselves from fraud and counterparty insolvencies."[5] That turned out to be total rubbish. It was the taxpayer who ended up picking up the bill for counterparty insolvencies, and the sums involved were and are huge.

As chance would have it, it was insurance against those very counterparty insolvencies which was to destroy AIG. This is a gigantic insurance company, worth $200 billion at its peak and definitely "too big to fail." It was AIG which was, in effect, the Joneses. It was the company which underwrote all the insurance: it was the single biggest player in the CDS market. Entertainingly for fans of financial acronyms, AIG was done in by CDSs on CDOs. That's to say, it took part in credit default swaps on collateralized debt obligations, the pools of subprime mortgages whose dramatic collapse in value in 2008 was the proximate cause of the financial crisis. When the investment bank Lehman Brothers imploded in September 2008, done in by its exposure to bad assets, there was a generalized panicked scramble to see who else was carrying similar risk. When it turned out that AIG was—and worse, that it was valuing those assets at much higher prices than Lehman Brothers had— investors freaked out and the company's credit rating collapsed. That meant that it had to post more collateral to cover its share of risk. In terms of the above example, the Joneses suddenly looked like a less safe risk, so the neighbors asked them to post more than the $10,000 of collateral against the loans—they wanted, and were contractually allowed to insist, that the Joneses now put up $20,000 for each $100,000 of risk they were covering. If the Joneses don't have that kind of money immediately at hand, they will have to borrow it. If they can't borrow it, they're toast.

And that's exactly what happened to AIG. When it had to increase its collateral cover, it couldn't, because the credit markets had tightened up. For the Joneses, that would be end of story: they'd be bankrupt. But because AIG was "too big to fail," the U.S. government stepped in with a bailout on September 16 worth $85 billion, in return for 79.9 percent of the company. (This bailout—they come in different varieties—was in the form of a twenty-four-month credit facility. To adopt an analogy to personal finances, that meant AIG could draw on the government's bank account.) On October 9, AIG was given another $37.8 billion in credit. Enough, already? No. On November 10, the U.S. Treasury pumped another $40 billion into the company by buying freshly issued stock created for the purpose (this being yet another variety of bailout—somebody should write a Bankster Bailout Cookbook). Finally enough, already? Don't be silly. On March 1, 2009, the Treasury gave the company another $30 billion and restructured the terms of its loan to make repayments of government money less arduous. The next day the company announced a loss for the quarter—not the year, the quarter—of $62 billion, the worst corporate results in history. Finally enough, already already? Not necessarily. According to the U.S. Treasury statement accompanying the fourth bailout, "Given the systemic risk AIG continues to pose and the fragility of markets today, the potential cost to the economy and the taxpayer of government inaction would be extremely high." To stabilize AIG would "take time and possibly further government support." That's what "too big to fail" means. You could put it like this: AIG + CDS + CDO + TBTF= $173,000,000,000.

In Britain, we had our entertaining but essentially distracting row over Sir Fred "Knighted for Services to Banking" Goodwin's pension; it's the similar outcry over bonuses paid to senior AIG executives after the bailouts. The bonuses totaled $165 million, and it doesn't take a PR professional to see that March 2009, after the fourth AIG bailout, wasn't the ideal time to have announced them. Everyone on both sides of American politics, from President Barack Obama downward, joined in the storm of outrage, which was followed by predictable bleating from the banksters. A Republican congressman invited the AIG executives to follow the "Japanese approach" and either apologize or commit suicide. (More authentic to do both, surely?) A Democratic senator threatened to tax the bonuses at 100 percent. *The New York Times* published an AIG executive's open letter to his boss, which said he was resigning because he hadn't been a derivatives trader and his feelings were hurt. He seemed to be expecting applause because he was repaying his own bonus of $742,006.40. Good fun all around. But the story was a distraction from the real scandal about AIG, which is what was happening to the other 99 percent of the money the government was pumping into the company. Since AIG wrote CDSs, which are effectively insurance against losses, and since those losses had occurred, why, then, was the money going to companies which had lost money in the credit crunch: companies such as Société Générale, which received $11.9 billion; Goldman Sachs, $12.9 billion; Merrill Lynch, $6.8 billion; Deutsche Bank, $11.8 billion; Barclays, $7 billion; BNP Paribas, $4.9 billion. Nothing could better illustrate the way in which this has become a systemic international crisis than the fact that the U.S. Treasury is transferring these gigantic sums to foreign banks, because it feels it has no choice if it's to keep the financial system functioning. But it's a hell of a pill for the U.S. taxpayer to have to swallow—one made much worse by the fact that Goldman Sachs went on, mere

months later, to declare record profits and pay record bonuses. AIG is broke, essentially because it got its sums
wrong about the level of risk represented by CDSs. So it
can't pay its counterparties (that's the other side of the insurance deal, the insurees). But the counterparties made the
same mistake, since they took out insurance with an insurer
which, in the event of a structural crisis, wouldn't be able
to afford to pay them. So why are the insurees walking
away whistling with pockets full of U.S. Treasury cash,
while the U.S. taxpayer sits on a gigantic loss? Note that
AIG's market capitalization—the total value of all its
shares—is no more than $2 billion. Saving the company
has cost eighty-five times as much as buying it would have.
Why, therefore, has the Treasury saved it? Because AIG is
"too big to fail." The implosion of Lehman Brothers in
September 2008 took what was already a crisis and very
nearly turned it into the total collapse of the global economic system: that was the point at which, in President
Bush's immortal words, "this sucker could go down." (Or,
as *The Onion* put it, "Bush calls for panic.') The lesson of
Lehman was, to politicians, crystal clear: it was that no financial institution of comparable size could ever again be
allowed to collapse. AIG was bailed out because it had the
entire economic system over a barrel.

Warren Buffett was doubly right to compare the new financial products to "weapons of mass destruction"—first,
because they are lethal, and, second, because no one knows
how to track them down. If the invention of derivatives
was the financial world's modernist dawn, the current crisis
is unsettlingly like the birth of postmodernism. For anyone
who studied literature in college in the past few decades,
there is a weird familiarity about the current crisis: value,
in the realm of finance capital, parallels the elusive nature

of meaning in deconstructionism. According to Jacques Derrida, the doyen of the school, meaning can never be precisely located; instead, it is always "deferred," moved elsewhere, located in other meanings, which refer and defer to other meanings—a snake permanently and necessarily eating its own tail. This process is fluid and constant, but at moments the perpetual process of deferral stalls and collapses in on itself. Derrida called this moment an "aporia," from a Greek term meaning "impasse." There is something both amusing and appalling about seeing his theories acted out in the world markets to such cataclysmic effect. It was CDSs which were the crucial instrument in making that happen, spreading risk throughout the financial system, not least because most of them are trading "over the counter," as it's called in the City—between one institution and another, with no intermediary. That means there is no central register of CDSs and no body capable of assessing and managing marketwide risks and where they are distributed.

As a direct corollary of that, there is no responsible body to check whether counterparties are actually in a position to pay the sums for which they are on the hook, should the insurance be called in. It's a severe case of caveat emptor, let the buyer beware—except actually, the buyer didn't need to beware, because the taxpayer was going to bail him out. So it emerged that the policy in fact was not so much "buyer beware" as "buyer, dude, don't bother bewaring, we've got this covered." Further compounding the potential problems was the fact that many of the risks were sold on and resold without the knowledge of the initial counterparty—which meant that a deal could end up being reinsured with the same banks more than once. As for the scale of those risks, well, they became huge. By June 2008, the International Swaps and Derivatives Association, or ISDA—the association of companies dealing in this stuff—was estimating the total size of the market as $54 trillion, close to the total GDP of the planet and many times more valuable than the total number of all the stocks and shares traded in the world. The underlying value of the risks being insured was much lower than the notional value, of course—but the lesson of Long-Term Capital Management was that when such deals blow up, they leave huge holes in the markets because of the sheer number of counterparties holding contracts with notional exposure to the risk. It's like a game of pass-the-parcel, in which nobody knows who's actually holding the parcel, much less what's going to be found inside it when it's unwrapped. So this tool, the CDS, which had been invented as a way of making lending safer, turned out to magnify and spread risks throughout the global financial system. It's as if people had used the invention of seat belts as an opportunity to take up drunk driving.

THREE

BOOM AND BUST

American urban desolation has a unique quality to it, once seen, never forgotten. My first encounter with it was in inner-city Detroit in 1996, and my main impression was of the crushing, oppressive emptiness of the streets. This wasn't just the ground-level vacancy that all high-rise buildings impose around them, this was another level of abandonment, desertion, flight—a science-fiction landscape, as in *I Am Legend*. The bleakness derives not just from Detroit's present but also from its history, and not just because of the way that history has been blighted by urban and racial politics gone horribly wrong, but also because of the straightforward way in which the history is one of descent and decline. Once, Detroit was prosperous; now it isn't. Once it was a pleasant place to live in; now it is dystopian. It's a model of what can go wrong with a city. Even amid decades of general prosperity and rising GDP, it is possible for a place to go as badly wrong, as far off the rails, as Detroit. [It might sound perverse, but the place it reminded me most of is Rome, in the long centuries after the ancient city's fall. It must have been a curious feeling to look not just at extraordinary things like the Colosseum but at the ordinary infrastructure of building and bridges and aqueducts, and accept that these were ruins of things which people had lost the ability to build. Detroit, especially its big buildings which once testified to civic optimism and aspiration, is like that.

I suppose it's partly because America is so rich that its poverty seems so bleak, so demoralized and demoralizing. But it's also that so many of the areas afflicted by modern poverty, and so many of the properties caught up in it, seen from another perspective, could be so pleasant to live in. There is a style of low-built row houses which feature in American cities, and which look from one point of view like ideal urban low-cost housing, built to a human scale and simply begging to be part of an idealized, mixed, diverse, complicated, modern way of living—it's as if the ideas of Jane Jacobs about the ideal patterns of neighborhood use and city life had been built into these streets from their inception. And it's that which makes them look so terrible when they go wrong. Because the houses are built to a pattern, small differences in upkeep, in the attention which all homes need, are magnified. Big differences are glaring. A house with a front porch that is falling down or that has boarded-up windows has the effect of dragging down the homes around it—and this isn't a matter just of aesthetics but of a now-proven pattern in sociology and urban development. The "broken windows," as they're called, drag down standards of behavior around them. When houses are completely unoccupied and can be broken into, they are an immediate magnet for vandals, crack smokers, firebugs, you name it; sometimes the power is cut off, sometimes the water, and sometimes one but not the other, leading to a simple and easy and devastating form of havoc for happy vandals—just turn on a tap and walk away.

I came to Baltimore because it is the subject of the only sustained work of art I've seen attempting to describe the lives lead in this urban desolation: David Simon's HBO series *The Wire*. From the point of view of writing about the housing crisis, it was almost an arbitrary choice. All across America a boom turned into a bust; foreclosures on housing loans are a pandemic. (The difference between a pandemic and an epidemic: a pandemic is everywhere at the same time.) This is one form of "deleveraging": the withdrawal of credit from people who often weren't in a position to repay it in the first place. It hit everywhere: Rust Belt cities, which had been struggling against population decline and associated problems for decades; Sunbelt areas, which had experienced sharp population growth in the new millennium, much of it from new migrants—the highest rate of repossession filings in the United States in the first six months of 2009 was in Nevada; exurbs sprawling out from urban areas all over the country; traditional boom-and-bust hot spots such as Florida. Some bizarre phenomena have been thrown up by the foreclosure crisis. One of the main players in the field is Deutsche Bank, which has been acting as trustee for the companies which own loans: this has led to a situation in which a German bank owns 10 percent of all the properties in Cleveland, Ohio. Deutsche Bank has been a major player in Baltimore, too, though the subprime crisis here is not so much an event in itself as the latest installment in a long-running and apparently endless series of misfortunes, some of them self-inflicted by the city and its inhabitants and some of them, like this one, not. So David Simon and his colleagues made a five-part, sixty-episode work of art—in effect a huge televised novel, which, as many observers have remarked, is Balzacian in its scope and achievement—and still managed to miss out on one of the worst disasters to affect Baltimoreans in decades. The credit crunch has cost 33,000 householders in Baltimore their properties, victims of the wave of mortgage foreclosures. This in a city where the population has in recent decades fallen from around a million to about 300,000 less, and where 50,000 homes were already lying unoccupied. As you drive around past block after block of abandoned properties, boarded up, some of them mere shells, some of them—some of the saddest—leaving one or two occupied houses behind in their wake, clinging bravely or desperately to what used once to be a decent place to live—it's hard not to think that this city looks as if it lost a war. It looked like that already before the credit crunch, but this city needed 33,000 home repossessions about as much as London needed the Luftwaffe during the Second World War.

The foreclosed now won't talk on the record about what's happened to them: too much litigation is under way, some of it directed by the city against the lenders behind the ensuing crisis. But you can talk to them off the record, and you can also go and look at some of the homes they've lost, such as 3803 Bonner Road in West Baltimore, a foreclosed loan from Wells Fargo that is now boarded up and covered in warning notices but would once have been a family home of proportions which aren't just generous but, by European standards, palatial. I wandered around outside, motivated by a curiosity which quickly gave way to sadness: there's just something so not-right about a big house, built for a big family, lying empty and abandoned and hauling the surrounding area slightly further downward as it sinks farther and farther into disrepair. And as for what will happen to the former inhabitants of this and the other 30,000 properties, that's even sadder. "I don't know, to be honest with you," Anthony DePastina, an attorney with the Baltimore nonprofit Civil Justice Network, a nonprofit legal organization involved in fighting for the foreclosed, told me.* "These thirty thousand essentially lost their homes because they can't make their mortgage payments. The reality is that they have little to no money. As a consequence of the mortgage foreclosure process their credit is ruined, so oftentimes rental companies aren't willing to rent to them because their credit is shot. So they either wind up moving in with other people that they know, a relative or friend, or if they're lucky they can rent a place on their own, either through a private landlord or a company that doesn't require a credit check. If they're very very unlucky, they wind up on the street."

I said, it's pretty bleak that people just disappear off the grid like that.

"Yes," he said. "The short answer is, nobody knows where they go. There is no safety net for these people. The social system is so strained at this time that it's very difficult to find appropriate housing in the same amount of time that you're being put out of your other house. I had a gentleman this morning, he's being put out of his home because he can't make his mortgage payments. We're anticipating that he'll be out of his home within ninety days. But he can't get on the waiting list to get assistance—the lady told him it could be up to a year, a year and a half. What does he do? He can't afford anything more than five hundred dollars a month, and he's the sole support of two children. There are thousands like him. I had another gen-

---

* Tony is also, we quickly and surprisedly worked out when we started discussing our Irish mothers, my third cousin.

tleman who was injured as a result of what's going to be a contested workplace injury. He was unable to work for a period, fell behind on his mortgage, lost his home. I personally spoke to three or four churches trying to get him help and several state agencies, but we couldn't raise him enough money to even get him into the most remedial apartment. He lived in his car for three or four months. He has no family, and currently he lives in what I would consider an abandoned trailer. He's trying to save his money to that he can get an apartment, but it takes time to get on his feet, it's probably going to take him another month or two. He's not looking to live in the Taj Mahal, he just wants a one-room apartment. So that's it. If they're lucky they get taken in by relatives, or they find a cash job and a renter who'll take them in for cash. But mainly, nobody knows."

And that's where the dream of owning your own home, combined with innovative new financial derivatives, has brought us. This is the other end of the causal chain behind the bank collapses and the seizing up of credit.

It's easy to lose money in the housing market. I've done it myself.

One of my most vivid memories of the late-1980s property bubble was how insanely boring it made so much conversation. There were dinner parties at which people spoke about literally nothing else, apart from the need to "get on the property ladder," about the inexorable rise in prices, about the fascinating new developments such as the exciting new go-go financial product, the endowment mortgage. (These were a much-touted product in which the borrower repaid only the interest of the loan directly to the mortgage company; the principal was repaid via investment in a guaranteed-to-succeed investment product, set to mature when the principal was due to be paid back. These products were the focus of a huge scandal when it turned out that—surprise!—they grew more slowly than predicted and failed to cover the principal amounts owed.) Margaret Thatcher had promised to create a "property-owning democracy," and by God, she was fulfilling her promise: during her time in office home ownership in the United Kingdom rose from 54 to 65 percent. In the process she proved Oscar Wilde wrong. He once said that the most frightening words in the English language were "I had a very interesting dream last night." Not true. In fact, the most frightening words in the language are "Did you hear how much they got for that house down the road?"

The single best thing about the bubble bursting in the late eighties was that all this went away. Half a million people lost their homes, which was horrible for them, but the good news was that for about a decade and a half, nobody talked about property prices anymore. That caused me to have a misanthropic, or unpatriotic, reflection: maybe one reason the British love talking about property prices so much is that it's one of the only times it's socially permissible to boast about how rich we are. For sure, and thank God, you hear a lot less about the value of people's houses when they're on the way down.

Why are we so obsessed? Take a step back, and there's nothing inherently interesting about the British property market. Say you bought your house in 1970 and paid the then national average price for it: £4,378. At the peak of the current spike in prices, that same house would have been worth £184,431. Congratulations! You've multiplied your money by forty-three times. You're rich, do you hear me? Rich! Except you aren't really. Strip out the effect of inflation, and that spectacular-sounding 4,300 percent price rise works out as 2.4 per percent a year in real terms. This is close, in other words, to the historic long-term average for investments regarded as being more or less without any risk at all. That's where the expression "safe as houses" comes from. Pick slightly different starting and finishing points, and the conclusions are pretty much the same— from 1973 to 2007, for instance, when inflation rates were different and prices were higher at the start and lower at the end: the result is 2.6 percent annual growth. That's more or less exactly the rate at which the whole British economy grew over the equivalent period. In other words, house prices performed exactly the same as the economy. So there's nothing interesting to say about them.

Life, however, isn't quite as simple as that. Yes, from a historic distance, the housing market is a dead safe, dead boring thing. Look at the graph of house prices, though, and it isn't like that. The overview shows steady, predictable progress; the close-ups show that house prices go up and down like a bride's nightie. When Gordon Brown promised us "an end to boom and bust," he was promising something no British politician has ever achieved. All markets overcorrect: they go too far on the way up, and then they go too far on the way down, which provides the momentum for them to go too far up again next time. With houses, for various reasons we'll get to in a moment, the ups and downs are worse.

I know—I've been there and done that. I bought my first flat in the autumn of 1987, egged on by the fact that everybody I knew was scraping every penny he or she had together to "get on the property ladder." The area was a bit of a dump, opposite King's Cross station, but I could walk to work and to pretty much anywhere else in London I wanted to go. The flat too was a bit of a dump, not least because it was so small. The shape of it was weird: already narrow to start with—for most of its length, I could reach both walls by stretching out my fingertips—it narrowed more at both ends. The American writer Madison Smartt Bell stayed downstairs at one point and used the flat as the basis of a novel about a man who goes mad, partly because his flat is such a strange shape.

The flat cost £59,000. Half of the money was money left to me when my father died, and the other half was borrowed from the Halifax. I repaid the interest and was advised to repay the principal using a miraculous new product called an endowment mortgage. Prices were rocketing. What could possibly go wrong?

I had many adventures in and around that flat. A period when I got on well with my landlord, who owned the freehold of the property, writing letters to his son's school for him, giving him unqualified advice about his insomnia, was followed by a falling-out in which he almost sued me and we didn't speak for three years. The man downstairs fell out with the landlord so badly he took an ax to the cupboard where the gas meter was, went to court to fight the service charge, lost, and sublet his flat out to two prostitutes. They fit in well with the rest of the area, which went downhill in the second Tory recession of the early nineties and filled up with drug dealers, prostitutes, pimps—and, worse, their customers. I learnt a lot about a lot of things through owning that flat.

What I didn't do was make any money. When I sold the flat, a decade later, it was for exactly what I had paid for it. That in real terms represented a loss of about 35 percent. It wasn't a surprise, because the property bubble had burst and flats around King's Cross were not an easy sell; when I asked the estate agents, which I did about every two years, they would sound shifty, ask what I'd paid for it, and then say that's about what they would expect to get. That wasn't true—what they meant was, you would be an idiot to sell. So I didn't.

And that was the most important thing I learnt from my first flat. Property prices go up and down, but the main thing is not to pay them a blind bit of notice, unless and until you have a good reason to move. I learnt that a rising price will not rise forever; that when prices stop rising, it will be difficult to sell your flat, because the reason the price has stopped rising is because the climate has changed. The money you have in your house is not liquid money; it's not money which can easily be converted into something else other than your house. It's stupid to feel richer because the value of your house has gone up, since the resulting rise almost always isn't money you can use or spend. If you're going to move, you still need somewhere to live, and the cost of that place too will have gone up, so there will be no net gain from the increase in your property's value.

I also learnt that although I hadn't made money, I hadn't lost it. That's because if you own a house, it effectively pays you an income—the money you would have spent in rent. My mortgage was a lot less than I would have spent in rent, so my flat was doing me economic favors, even while its price was flatlining. Finally, thanks to that endowment mortgage, I learnt not to put too much trust in anything I was told by the economic services industry. (Because I was missold the policy so early, I'm not covered by the compensation scheme that the industry was belatedly and grudgingly forced to bring in from 1989.)

The fact is that for many people, the ups and downs on the charts, the spikes and troughs, each represents a manic-depressive roller coaster. The ups are the bubbles and the downs are the crashes, and it is the recurrence of these which makes the U.K. housing market so distinctive; which in turn brings us back again to the question, why? Why are we so obsessed with our properties and their price?

That question has both a short answer and a long one. The long one concerns the fundamental structural differences of the U.K. property market. So many of us own our own homes: 70 percent of the British population live in their own home. The number has continued to go up since Margaret Thatcher, as successive governments have continued her pro-ownership policies. This is a much higher figure than in comparable economies in Europe: for instance, only 40 percent of Germans own their own home. Many, many things flow from that fact.

The first is to do with that small word "own." In practice, most of us own our home through a mortgage, which means that we don't own our home at all. Back in the days of my first flat, you didn't even hold the property deed of your own property if you had a mortgage: the bank held the deed. There was something brutal about that, but at least the point was stark: if you have a mortgage, you don't own your own home, and it's a good idea to remember the fact.

If you have a mortgage, though, your life is in thrall to a number: the interest rate. In continental Europe, policy wonks and bankers care what the interest rate is, but no one else does. Here, the interest rate has the potential to dominate your life. This is the single biggest reason why the United Kingdom has not joined the euro—because the British economy has cycles which aren't exactly in phase with Europe's and because the interest rate has such a directly personal effect on people's finances here. If we had joined the euro and our mortgages had been tied to those groovily low euro interest rates, money would have been even cheaper and credit even more easily available, so the housing bubble would have been even bigger and the crash correspondingly crashier. (Two examples of countries where that happened: Ireland and Spain.) The credit crunch has exposed significant problems with the running of the European Central Bank, the body which, in essence, runs the euro. But the ECB has a Europe-wide theater in which to operate, and there are sure to be times when the concerns of its member countries will vary sharply. Ireland and Spain desperately needed a spike in interest rates to pop their respective bubbles, but under the leadership of the head of the ECB, Jean-Claude Trichet, that simply isn't the bank's mandate. The result was the grotesque bubble and the horrific crash which inevitably ensued in both countries. The range of competing needs to be juggled by the ECB is just too diverse: the demands of a car manufacturer in Düsseldorf who is worried about wage inflation can't be squared with those of a Latvian restaurateur who needs to borrow capital or a Spanish financier worried about economic overheating. The European Union's lack of a single political boss, or a single electorate, is a further difficulty.

So that's the first thing that's different about British mortgages: there are more of them. Second, they are bigger: the size of the loan is proportionately bigger in relation to the value of the house. German banks, for instance, will lend only a maximum of 60 percent of a property's value. In France, the rules are even more strict. For a start, our model of the mortgage, in which the loan is keyed to the value of the house being bought, doesn't apply. In France, it's the other way around. The critical figure is not the value of your property but the size of your income. Banks have to lend only the money you can reasonably afford to pay back out of your monthly pay packet. In practice, that figure has been assessed as being a third of your income. So a bank will only lend a third of what you're earning—and if the bank stretches the rules and you get into trouble paying the money back, the bank can be sued for reckless lending. It's the bank which bears the responsibility for your not borrowing stupid amounts of money.

Linked to this is the fact that attitudes to debt are different. For instance, in France, you can write a check without any additional ID, but if that sounds as if it implies a happy-go-lucky, carefree attitude to money, the exact opposite is true: you don't need ID because it is a criminal offense to write a check for more money than you have in your account. (It's a bit like French libel law. The amounts of money awarded in French libel cases are tiny—not because the French don't care about their reputations but because they do. The point of honor is sufficient in itself. Contrast this to Britain, with our ridiculously crook-friendly libel law and huge cash awards—if anybody cared about the point of alleged honor, the cash wouldn't be necessary.) Add this together, and you get an entirely different culture of money, borrowing, and debt, one which means that the French have dramatically lower levels of household debt than the Anglo-Saxon economies. In Britain, going into the credit crunch, the typical household owed more than 160 percent of its average income—an alarmingly high figure and one which reflects our high levels of mortgage debt, and general willingness to borrow, borrow, borrow in order to spend, spend, spend. In France the equivalent figure was 60 percent. Individually and collectively, French households are much less stretched and much less at risk from a downturn. Economists attribute this to the fact that Germany and France were the first countries to emerge officially from the current recession.

Back in the days of my first mortgage, British loans were like European ones, in that the bank preferred not to lend you more than half, or at the most three-quarters, of the value of the property. They also preferred not to lend you more than two and a half times your annual income; if two of you were buying a property together, you could stretch to three times your joint income. Back in those days it was very hard, verging on impossible, for people who do what I do now—write for a living—to get a mortgage, because we couldn't produce the relevant pay slips and employment history.*

All those rules have long since gone from the U.K. property market. A banker involved in picking over the corpse of Northern Rock told me, "Most of the loans were sound, but one or two of their books had blown up, and one of the worst of them was the hundred and twenty percent mortgages." I asked why anyone would want to borrow 120 percent of the value of the thing they were buying, and he just shrugged. That product makes sense only if you are

---

* These days it's different—or was until the credit crunch—and writers can get mortgages, the same as everyone else. But some areas are still harder and/or more expensive for writers, and one of them is car insurance. Writers' premiums are significantly higher than those of regular citizens. I asked a mortgage broker why this is: is it because novelists are supposed to be drunk all the time and prone to crashing into things? His reply: "Yeah, partly, but it's more that you'll write a book, and it'll be a big success, like *Bridget Jones* or something, and then they'll make it into a film and you'll meet Renée Zellweger and then you'll be driving around with her and have an accident and she'll go through the windscreen of your car and the insurance company will have to compensate her for loss of earnings. That's what they're really worried about."

absolutely certain of the value of the property you're buying: and there is no reason to be absolutely certain of that. We have these crazily risky, heavily leveraged mortgages, and Europeans don't. Also, they borrow for shorter periods, a decade or twenty years at most, as opposed to the twenty-five or thirty years that is standard in Britain. It is also much harder for Europeans to remortgage. All these reasons, taken together, are why Europeans are more likely to rent than to own. In turn, it means that we are borrowing much more money, for longer, at much greater risk.

Another feature of the U.K. mortgage market adds to that risk: the fact that we prefer to pay our mortgages at variable rates. The United States has a home ownership rate similar to that of the United Kingdom: more mortgages, for a higher proportion of the property value and with longer repayment periods. In the United States, though, far more of the loans are at fixed interest rates. British householders are allergic to fixed interest rates; we prefer variable-rate loans. No one quite knows why, since fixed interest rates often make good sense and have the effect of transferring some of the risk of the loan to the banks. If you have a variable-rate mortgage and the central bank interest rate goes up, you feel it in your pocket; if you have a fixed-rate mortgage and the same thing happens, the bank feels it. In the United States the two institutions designed to help the banking system to bear the risk of this fixed-rate lending are Fannie Mae and Freddie Mac; and the reason they went under was precisely because they were swamped by the cost of these risks.

The lack of these products in other countries reflects the historic differences in attitudes to property. I have a theory about why we are like this: our longing is connected to the sense of dislocation which spread throughout British society during the industrial revolution. If we for a moment ignore what we already know about property and imagine what property markets in different countries might be like—if we think counterfactually—then it might seem logical for things to be the other way around. Countries with a go-go attitude to the free market, countries which pride themselves on their openness to competition, willingness to take a chance, lack of featherbedding, and protection from the laws of the jungle, might be expected to have a property market in which people were easygoing about renting and reluctant to tie up all their money in a single illiquid asset. On the other hand, countries with more traditional, less capitalistic attitudes, less open to the cold winds of the markets and more willing to protect their citizens from market realities, might well have a conservative appetite for bricks and mortar. Instead it's the other way around. Why? Well, perhaps that's exactly why. It's precisely the most free-market, go-go countries which show this overpowering appetite for people to own their own homes. The less security there is in the workplace, the more exposed the rest of life is to the pressures of competition and uncertainty, the more people want to feel secure within their own four walls, at the beginning and end of the harsh working day. Britain was the first country to experience the transforming impact of industrial life and the associated disconnections among land and labor and place. Just as the industrial revolution broke the food culture of Britain, it created a new emphasis on the distinction between the industrialized workplace and the private space of home. The huge expansion in British home ownership began during the 1840s, when the effects of the industrial revolution had spread sufficiently to create a new middle class with the economic means to buy their own homes. Because we were alienated and insecure at work, we felt an increased need to own the walls we live in; to feel safe and in possession of our own property. It was the psychic trade-off for the other losses of industrialization.

All those factors taken together add up to the reason why the U.K. housing market is different. They are the long answer to the question "why?" But the short answer is different. If you try to ask why these factors arose—why it is that our mortgages and hence our market are different— you end up with this answer: nobody knows. The investment products which allow people to own homes in Britain are different from those elsewhere because they grew up to answer a need that is different: our obsessive need to own our own homes. Our risky, long-term, innovative (sometimes recklessly so) mortgages came into existence because the market set out to find ways to let us fulfill our heart's deepest desire, to own our own property. The appetite created the products, not the other way around.

———

The broad distinction is that in some countries, home ownership is regarded as a good thing but not an essential. If you can afford it and if you prefer owning to renting, then by all means own your own home. If you can't afford it or temperamentally don't want to be tied down by a long-term, highly leveraged, highly illiquid investment, then so what, you rent. In other countries, however, home ownership is an unquestioned primary good. It implies safety, prosperity, full participation in society. Owning your own home could almost be seen as a fundamental right. It follows that in these countries, governments will pursue policies designed to increase home ownership. The United Kingdom and United States are two of those countries.

This isn't exclusively, or even primarily, a preoccupation

of the political left. In Britain, it was Margaret Thatcher who spoke of a vision of a "property-owning democracy" and who, more energetically than any other modern politician, pursued policies designed to increase the level of home ownership, extending mortgage tax relief and introducing a new right for council-house tenants to buy their own homes. There was a strong political tinge to these ideas, involving the belief that home owners were—to put it bluntly—more likely to be both small c and big C conservative. In America, it was the unlikely figure of Herbert Hoover who began the drive to create government policies favoring home ownership.[1] Hoover would later be a model of complacent conservatism at its sleepiest, which is why it's all the odder that he saw home ownership as such a crusade. He was apparently motivated by the 1920 census, which showed a tiny drop in the percentage of home owning from 45.9 to 45.6 percent since 1910. This, thought Hoover, was a disaster. "Nothing is worse than increased tenancy and landlordism," he argued. The parallel with Margaret Thatcher's views about the virtues of home ownership, more than half a century later, are clear, though Hoover expressed his opinions more fruitily. "The home owner has a constructive aim in life. . . . He works harder outside his home, he spends his leisure hours more profitably, and he and his family live a finer life and enjoy more of the comforts and cultivating influences of our modern civilization." On the other end of the political spectrum, they would have put it differently, but they basically agreed. In the words of *The New York Times* on the decline in home ownership revealed by the 1920 census, "The nation's stability [is] being undermined. . . . The masses [are] losing their struggle for a better life."

The result was a decades-long emphasis on policies

designed to increase home ownership, beginning with Hoover's Own Your Own Home campaign and continuing through the Home Owners' Loan Corporation, which bailed out troubled mortgage borrowers during the Great Depression, and the creation of Fannie Mae and Freddie Mac. With home ownership established as a political good and a government mechanism created to extend home ownership through the decades of prosperity which followed World War II—decades which had their ups and downs but which nonetheless saw a general upward movement in living and working conditions—everything was hunky-dory. Or almost everything. The trouble with near-universal increases in prosperity is in that small word "near." From the 1960s onward, there was clear and growing evidence that specific sectors of the community, especially ethnic minorities, were discriminated against in the way the mortgage industry worked, not in theory but in practice. Behavior such as "redlining"—drawing a red line around certain neighborhoods and refusing to lend money to their residents—came under well-deserved attack. Pressure grew for the government—which after all, thanks to Fannie and Freddie, was the single biggest player in the mortgage market—to correct this inequality.

The campaign achieved some of its aims when the first President Bush signed off on legislation to force Fannie Mae and Freddie Mac to make sure that 30 percent of their loans went to borrowers with low and moderate incomes. President Clinton's housing secretaries, first Henry Cisneros and then Andrew Cuomo, set out to execute policies which would extend housing ownership among groups which had historically been excluded from it. There had been a number of changes over the previous decades, which came together to make new forms of lending possible. In 1980, the Depository Institutions Deregulation and Monetary Control Act, or DIDMCA, made it legal to charge higher rates and fees to some borrowers, which was the very definition of a subprime loan. In 1982, the Alternative Mortgage Transaction Parity Act, or AMPTA, made it legal to charge variable interest rates and arrange for "balloon payments" to catch up the unpaid balance at the end of a loan, and then the Tax Reform Act of 1986, or TRA, allowed the tax deduction of interest on mortgage loans, immediately and dramatically increasing their appeal as a form of debt. So a new category of lending already existed, conjured into being by changes in the law under administrations and congresses of both political flavors. The Clinton administration continued in this direction, giving the existing policy a strong but inexplicit racial edge: the preferred euphemism was to speak of "underserved" communities. As for the things which could be done differently to target the previously excluded, the innovations included making it possible to borrow the full value of a house, without a deposit; deemphasizing credit history and instead saying that if a would-be borrower was paying rent and utility bills, he or she could be considered for a loan; allowing borrowers to claim seasonal employment and financial assistance as income; and raising the limit of mortgages which could qualify for protection from the government. Because Fannie Mae and Freddie Mac were strange officially-private-but-really-public hybrid corporations, the government was able to get what it wanted in this area of mortgage policy—and the reason it was able to do so was that mortgage lenders began to see the new field of lending to low-income borrowers as a huge area for potential growth. Obviously these loans had to be assessed carefully, on a case-by-case basis; but as long as that happened, the new loans were a thing of beauty. American home ownership increased to a historic high of 68.9 percent, and the gap between ethnic minorities and the white (or "non-Hispanic white" as the U.S. Census data term it) population narrowed: between 1994 and 2005 white home ownership increased by 8.3 percent, African American by 13.6 percent, and Hispanic by 20.1 percent. From the point of view of encouraging home ownership, the policies were working. The borrowers wanted money, the government wanted them to have the money, the lenders wanted to make money, and everybody could get what they wanted.

Home prices go up and down and in the long run, the evidence says, don't grow any faster than the rest of the economy, plus inflation. That makes sense if you think about it—why should they grow any faster? The whole industry of hype and bubble building and kerfuffle around property investing is based on ignoring this boring truth. That doesn't mean that people don't make and lose fortunes in property during the spikes and jags of the market; but in the long run and on aggregate, the research is clear. The best way to make money with investments, over a long term, is through shares; or, as they are known in financial-speak, equities. (A sometimes overlooked but essential component of this has to do with the dividends, the regular payments the company makes to its shareholders.) Compared with the effect of holding money in property or a bank account, the long-term advantages of investment in equities are obvious. At least, that's what the historic data show. But the time scale of the data are crucial: we're talking about minimum periods of five years at a time. In the shorter run, as everybody knows, share prices go up and down like a gorilla on a pogo stick.

With bonds—which, remember, are the other main way in which companies raise money and fund themselves—it's a little different. Share prices are like the weather, choppy and variable. Bond prices are more like a sea swell, slower and more gradual and with a momentum which is impossible to ignore or contradict. The biggest single influence on them is the government-determined interest rate: the rate at which the government is willing to lend short-term money to financial institutions to keep the economy running. This rate is set by the Federal Reserve in the United States and by the Bank of England in the United Kingdom, and it is this rate which in turn determines the rate at which banks lend money to one another, and then to businesses, and then to us. So although the chairman of the Fed doesn't barge into your bank manager's office and tell him how much your mortgage should cost, actually, he sort of does. This interest rate is critical to the economy in all sorts of respects. In fact, in terms of how the economy is functioning, it is the single most important number, because it is the interest rate which determines how much money costs.

This point is so familiar to the economically literate that they don't bother to explain it to the rest of us: money does not always cost the same. There are times when money is expensive: the late 1970s and early '80s, for instance, when the U.K. interest rate peaked at 17 percent and the U.S. rate at 20 percent. When money is expensive, the economy tends to slow down, unemployment rises, consumer spending slows, it is harder for businesses to raise money, it is harder to make money on the stock market because everyone is eyeing the attractive interest rates they can get elsewhere. Inflation—which involves money being worth less over time—comes under severe pressure from the fact that money is more expensive in the present. And as for the bond market, the main way in which companies raise money, the effect is impossible to exaggerate. If U.S. government Treasury bills, the securest investment in the world, are paying 20 percent for no risk at all, what sort of interest rates would you have to offer customers to get them to buy your company's pesky bonds? Answer: incredibly high ones. And if your bond was issued a few years ago and pays only a paltry 5 percent, what will have happened to its price? Answer: it will be, as traders so elegantly put it, in the toilet. On the other hand, if the interest rate is low and money is cheap, there is the risk of inflation—of money losing its value over time—but on the other hand it's easy for companies to raise money, the economy will pick up speed, and so will consumer spending. Employment will rise. It will suddenly be cheaper for companies to issue new bonds, so existing bonds with higher rates of interest will spike in value. Notice that both these states are, or should be, self-correcting. High interest rates will slow things down and gradually bring inflation down, which in turn will exert downward pressure on interest rates; low interest rates, which governments use to boost the economy, will heat things up in a way which causes inflation and leads to a rise in the interest rate. So the movement is self-correcting in both directions.

Stocks and bonds are the two biggest single fields of global investment, reaching into every corner of economic life. At the beginning of the new millennium, however, both of them were going through an odd patch. The stock market had undergone a spectacular bubble in Internet and new-economy stocks. Some of what was happening seemed to belong to a classic hysteria equal to that of the great historical bubbles such as the Dutch tulip mania, the South Sea bubble, or the nineteenth-century bubble in railway stocks. The broad rules of these bubbles and implosions are well known. They were first systematized by the economist Hyman Minsky, and their best-known popular formulation is in the classic text by Charles P. Kindleberger, *Manias, Panics, and Crashes: A History of Financial Crises*. The basic pattern of these manias is that a real phenomenon comes along (overseas exploration, railways, the Internet), is latched onto by investors, is blown out of all proportion, and continues surging upward anyway, so more investors pile in on the basis of what's now called "greater fool theory." I vividly remember the first time I heard this term, on the lips of one of the cleverest people I've ever met, explaining why he had invested heavily in what were obviously hugely overvalued technology stocks. He told me what he'd done, I said I thought he was nuts, and then he explained the "greater fool theory." What it means is that even though everyone knows that what's happening is crazy, there's still money to be made by buying stocks and selling them a little while later to the eponymous "greater fool." So it doesn't matter how overvalued the stocks are, as long as there is a bigger idiot out there willing to buy them from you, you've made a nice profit. It works—until it stops working. Historically, what happens is that the bubble starts to wobble, often in response to a piece of bad news, and people begin to express doubts; then everything abruptly collapses and everybody loses an enormous amount of money. That's exactly what happened with the bubble in technology stocks. It burst in March 2000, and the Nasdaq index of technology stocks fell by 80 percent. The dot-com crash wiped out $5 trillion of investors' money and came to be known as one of the greatest destructions of capital in history.

When there are stock market busts, investors for a period turn cool toward equities. This is no surprise, and, historically, crashes of this sort almost always uncover frauds and malfeasances of a type which had escaped everyone's notice while prices were rising. Downturns put pressure on earnings, and companies which are less than wholly honest begin to creak at the seams; at the same time, the voices which have been warning that there is something funny about Charles Ponzi (in 1920), Ivar Kreuger the match king (in 1932), Bernie Ebbers (in 2002), or Bernard Madoff (in 2008) begin to gain a hearing. The decline in share prices rolls over a rock, and an unsettling variety of financial beasties emerge. In the case of the millennial dot-com bust, the creature which came crawling out from underneath the rock was a fraud so spectacular and so systematic and so magnificently, reekingly wrong that it was in its way almost a thing of beauty: Enron.

To fully understand the impact that Enron had, you have to appreciate just how admired the company was in its prime. *Fortune* magazine has an award for the most innovative company in the United States. Enron won it in every year from 1995 to 2000. Its annual revenues reached $101 billion. It had interests in everything from paper and broadband to natural gas and its core business, electricity, and it traded extensively in derivatives in all those areas.* Much of its profits were registered via the company's enthusiastic adoption of "mark-to-market" accounting, which—in Enron's interpretation, anyway—allowed it to

---

* If you live in the West Country of England, you have literally drunk Enron's water. The Texas-based fraudsters bought Wessex Water in 1998, a disastrous investment as it turned out, because the wave of deregulation in the industry caused the price of water to drop—not through competition, as free marketers would tell us to expect, but because the regulators insisted on bringing the price down.

account as current profits deals for which the revenues were due to come in some distance in the future. Thus a long-term contract to buy gas over a period of many years could be booked right now, today, as current profits.[2] In addition, Enron created an extensive array of external companies off its own balance sheets and sold assets to those companies at artificially inflated prices. Basically, it bought things from itself at made-up prices. All of these tricks kept the share price zooming upward. When an analyst raised concerns about the balance sheet during a conference call, the company's CEO, Jeffrey Skilling, said, "Well, thank you very much, we appreciate that . . . asshole." (The call was taped and now features on lists of "top ten CEO outbursts.") Except that the asshole was right: Enron's accounting was so corrupt that when the nature of the frauds came out, the share price crashed from $90 to nothing, Skilling went to jail for twenty-four years, the auditor Arthur Andersen (one of the world's five biggest accountancy firms) was put out of business, many employees lost their life savings, and many investors' sentiments turned sharply against the stock market, since if a much-admired, much-analyzed blue-chip investment such as Enron could turn out to be worth nothing, whose accounts could you trust?* The economist Robert Shiller regularly sends out a questionnaire to investors, and the response in 2001, after the Enron crash, was that "Investors told us in no uncertain terms that the accounting scandals were a major factor in their withdrawal from the stock market."

As a result of the dot-com crash and the Enron implo-

---

* "Blue chip" is a term originally from poker: blues are the highest-denomination chips. Hence the term's use for the biggest companies on the stock market.

sion, the early years of the new millennium were a time when the money which chases the new idea, the go-go idea, had turned its attention away from the stock market.

The traditional bond market, also, was not a place to seek the next new thing. The reason was simple: interest rates were, by historic standards, unusually low. Alan Greenspan, the head honcho of U.S. monetary policy during the Clinton years, had presided over a period of economic growth during which the U.S. economy seemed to have achieved a highly desirable "Goldilocks point" of being neither too hot nor too cold, so that it kept growing without causing inflation. (Economists sometimes call this period of regular, noninflationary, non-boom-and-bust growth "the Great Moderation." The term was coined by Greenspan's successor, Ben Bernanke.) When the dot-com crash came, the fear was that the stock market bust would spread into the rest of the economy and bring it grinding to a halt; so Greenspan responded by cutting interest rates. Non-American readers may wonder what this has to do with them. The answer is twofold. One, the U.S. economy is the biggest in the world, and to a large extent it drives world output and the world economy. Two, the U.S. dollar is what is known as the world's reserve currency: it is the currency in which a majority of other countries save money and also the currency in which a number of global commodities such as oil and coffee (the world's number one and number two most traded commodities) are priced. The dollar interest rate is not the planetary interest rate, but in many respects it comes close. In May 2000, the U.S. federal funds rate was 6.5 percent; Greenspan cut it and kept cutting. Then 9/11 happened, and for a time it seemed as if the entire world order were teetering on its axis. Translated into the language of the economy and markets, that meant uncertainty; and if there is one thing which markets and economies hate, it is uncertainty. Greenspan surveyed this landscape, took in the imminence of war and the certainty of sharply spiking oil and commodity prices at a time of what looked like a general slowdown, and made what with the benefit of hindsight was a major mistake: he continued to cut interest rates. This process carried on until June 2003, when the rate hit 1 percent, exceptionally low by historic standards. It stayed at that level way into 2004.

The low interest rates meant that it was easy for businesses to raise money cheaply; and also easy for consumers to borrow money; and also easy for construction companies to raise money; and also easy for borrowers to take out mortgages. Bond prices stayed low: by historic standards, very low. I've said that this would normally be a self-correcting phenomenon. Because bonds were giving low yields, buyers would drift away from them; because buyers were drifting away, bonds would have to increase their yields to attract them back. Here, though, a new factor entered the equation. Economists are arguing about this phenomenon and how important it was—Alan Greenspan himself has attributed the entire bubble and crash to it—but the broad outline is apparent and can be summed up in a single word: China. The Chinese economy had boomed, and China had effectively become the factory for the developed world, making pretty much everything. (A brief check on my immediate surroundings: my underpants, socks, trousers, and T-shirt, and the shiny Apple laptop on which I'm typing these very words, were all made in China.) As a result of these export earnings, China was awash with money. And what did it do with that money? A democratic country would have faced strong pressures to take the hundreds of billions of yuan flowing into the country and

invest them in roads, schools, hospitals, research, infrastructure, medicine, higher pay for state employees, higher
levels of benefits, you name it. A nondemocratic country
doesn't have to face the same pressures; not in the same
way. China took its huge trade surplus and invested, hugely,
in the United States—specifically, in U.S. government debt.
China bought U.S. Treasury bills to the tune of $699 bil-
lion; and that accounts for just the explicit purchases of
T-bills, not the numerous other investments China made in
dollar-based securities and bonds. So rather than spend its
own money, China chose to fund America's spending. One
can argue about just how much of the credit bubble can be
attributed to that, but the basic phenomenon is clear. Chinese factories kept down inflation by keeping goods cheap
at a time when prices would normally have begun to rise;
Chinese investments kept the U.S. government able to borrow money cheaply and spend more, at a time when that
borrowing would normally have become more expensive.
It bought T-bills, and kept on buying them, at a time when
their low yield would normally have kept investors away—
which would in turn have driven up the yield that T-bills
were paying.

So low interest rates were bad for the bond market. But
there was one place where they were pure catnip: the housing market. It was cheaper than ever to raise the money to
buy yourself a first house, if you didn't already have one, or
a bigger and better house if you already did. It had never
been cheaper or easier to borrow money. With all this credit
around, house prices began to go up. This is called "asset
price inflation," and, simply put, it means that instead of
stock prices going up (which they weren't much, in the aftermath of the dot-com crash) or bond prices going up
(which they weren't much because interest rates were so

low), other categories of assets go up in price instead. What's most people's single biggest asset? Their home. With low interest rates, the entire developed world began to experience a run-up in home prices. In the decade up to 1995, U.S. home prices went up by 57.7 percent, British ones by 134.7 percent, Irish by 242 percent, Spanish by 114 percent. That got a lot of moneymen thinking about how to profit from the new boom in housing prices.

FOUR

ENTER THE GENIUSES

This is one of those points when it helps to see capital as an agent, a force in its own right. So let's ask ourselves what, at this point, capital would have wanted, if it could have its own way. Assume that capital is like a virus and its motivation is to replicate; it wants to grow. The return on equities is at a low. The return on bonds is at a low. So capital begins to seek innovative ways of growing and replicating. If the old formulas aren't working, money will seek new formulas.

Not much is going on in stocks and bonds. (Apart from the many trillion dollars' worth of them which change hands every day, obviously—what I mean is, not much new or out of the ordinary.) Where things are going on is in the property market. There, prices are zooming up. An enormous amount of money is therefore piling into the mortgage market. That, from capital's point of view, is good news, because mortgages offer a steady stream of repayment money, as well as the potential to take part in the increase in home values as property prices steadily rise. Also, even when interest rates are low, mortgage rates are that little bit less low: we homeowners pay more for our borrowing than governments or companies do. At this point we can imagine capital sticking its head up, its nose twitching, sensing that it might here be onto something.

But it gets better. In this property boom, all sorts of people who have for years been sitting on the sidelines are now wanting to buy homes, to share in the dream of security and prosperity and inclusion which is represented by home ownership. The great thing about these new entrants to the property market is that they have no history of home ownership and not much other record of financial good citizenship; they have lousy credit ratings. Fantastic! That means they have to pay more when they borrow. Because they are assessed as bad risks, they pay more to take out mortgages. That means that their debt gives a wonderfully high yield; and at a time when the yields of everything else are disappointingly low, that makes them the answer to capital's whispered prayer.

Somebody had long since worked out a way of making collateralized debt obligations out of mortgages, the same way that they had out of corporate debt and bonds and suchlike. Remember, a collateralized debt obligation is a pool of debt being paid back by a group of borrowers, which is added together and then sold on a set of bonds paying a range of different interest rates. Collateralized debt obligations, which had begun with corporate forms of debt, now moved into the area of mortgage holders paying off their mortgages. As always, there would be two streams of revenue, one from the fees to set up the deal and another from the repayments themselves.

Up until now, these mortgage-backed CDOs had been made up only from what was called "conforming" mortgages. Fannie Mae and Freddie Mac had rules about who could be lent money and under what terms. Mortgages which conformed to those rules were known as "conforming loans." The mortgage lenders in between Fannie and Freddie and the general public—remember, F and F don't lend directly to the public but to the financial institutions which actually own the mortgages—had even more rules. There were restrictions based on credit history, on the amount of the full house price that could be lent to the borrower, and so on. Now, though, there was a huge new market in "nonconforming" mortgages which didn't fit Fannie and Freddie's criteria. Mortgage lending to "underserved" communities was a principled policy which had been ingeniously executed by a careful extension of the mortgage-lending criteria to lower-income, higher-risk groups. The policy seemed to work, and it did not take mortgage lenders long to realize what that meant: that there was a new market in riskier and therefore more lucrative lending to be found among poorer and apparently less creditworthy borrowers. So mortgage lenders, first cautiously and then with increasing enthusiasm, began extending their lending to this new class of creditors. These "nonconforming" mortgages were also known as "subprime" mortgages, a name which was confusing in one respect, because "subprime" mortgages paid a higher rate of interest than prime ones. From the point of view of capital, "subprime" was better because it paid out more. So if someone could work out a way of designing a CDO based on these sexy subprime mortgages . . .

It would be perfect. And again the power of securitization would do its magic work. That process of securitization and selling on would free up more capital for more lending. Except for one slight problem, which is that it was impossible. The reason it was impossible was because of an apparently insuperable statistical problem. In the corporate world which underpinned the already thriving global market in CDOs, there was a huge amount of evidence, statistics, and history underpinning the deals that were made. All the evidence for corporate histories of interest rates, repayments, defaults, the whole kaboodle, was publicly known. In fact it wasn't just known, it was pored over, sweated over, broken down, and analyzed, and the process of doing so was the whole function of some of the most important agencies in the financial world, the credit-rating agencies, Moody's and S&P's and the rest. Assessing default rates and the security of bonds was their raison d'être, it was why they got up in the morning. The default rate was a particular crux for the credit-rating agencies, because default rates can have such a huge impact on the quality of a loan: if you make ten loans and one of them goes bad, that bad loan is likely to wipe out all your profits from the other nine good bets. So there was an entire industry devoted to studying the underlying pools of debt which went into CDOs.

Regular vanilla, plain-Jane mortgages were, broadly speaking, similar. If you had large numbers of respectable citizens with good credit histories, it wasn't too hard to model the risks involved when it came to designing CDOs. But subprime mortgages were different. There simply weren't the same pools of data available on how they performed, since they had popped into existence only about ten minutes before. Another big issue was that the United States was regarded not as a single housing market, in the way that in most countries housing markets are a single entity. The United States consisted of dozens of different local markets, which behaved according to local differences, local demographic patterns, local booms and busts. Some states had steady property markets. Others, such as Florida, were famous for cyclical episodes of bubbles and crashes (often linked to lurid, spectacular, only-in-Florida frauds). It was hard to be sure—because the data were local and patchy and had never been properly collected or correlated—but it seemed likely that there had never been a national property crash in the United States. That's to say that although there had been innumerable ups and downs in specific markets, the national housing market had never gone down in its entirety.

The risk assessments of lenders are based on statistics. Particular scenarios are modeled, and then the effect on loans is measured and analyzed. But how was it possible to do that with so little data? How could you assess the effect of a national downturn in house prices? The problem in particular was one of correlation. This is a term in statistics which is close enough to its regular English usage to be accessible to common sense. Just how could anyone assess the risks of things—in particular house price crashes and defaults—happening to different people at different places? Correlations were a much-studied feature of the stock market and could be used to hedge and to reduce risk. It was a huge help to know which stocks moved together and which moved in different or opposite rhythms. If banks knew how to correlate subprime mortgages—how to build models to assess probabilities—they would feel much safer about building credit derivatives out of them.

And then, bingo, somebody did it. David X. Li was a math jock from rural China. If the credit crunch had been a novel by John le Carré, Robert Ludlum, or, for that matter, Stendhal, he would be the central character: shadowy but determined, a true international man of mystery. Adding to the mystery is the fact that no one now knows where he is. Li had been sent to North America on a government scholarship in the late 1990s to learn about capitalism. (That's a period detail in itself: the time can't be far away when students keen to study capitalism will be piling onto planes to Shanghai.) In the process he acquired four degrees, the first in economics from Nankai, the second an MBA from Quebec, the third and fourth, both from the university of Waterloo in Ontario, a master's in actuarial sciences and a Ph.D. in statistics. Then he went to work, at first for the Canadian Imperial Bank of Commerce (a name which might well be what Oscar Wilde called the Royal Irish Academy, "a triple oxymoron"). In 2000, while working at J.P. Morgan, Li managed to apply a piece of mathematics called a Gaussian copula function to the creation of CDOs. This is what the math looks like:*

$$C_\rho(u, \upsilon) = \Phi_\rho \left(\Phi^{-1}(u), \Phi^{-1}(\upsilon) \right)$$

I have absolutely no idea what any of that means, but in plain English it is a way of modeling lots of different things happening in different ways at the same time. The formula was already much used in statistics; Li found a way of applying it to the world of CDOs and published the result in *The Journal of Fixed Income* (which is basically *Zoo* or *Heat* for the CDO market), in a paper called "On Default Correlation: A Copula Function Approach." He had found the Great White Whale of the CDO market, a way to correlate the apparently uncorrelatable—and thus had opened up the whole field of subprime loans as a source of CDOs.

As we've already seen via the story of the Black-Scholes equation, the markets are not slow to pick up on innova-

---

* From Wikipedia, which has its flaws but is brilliant on science.

tions of this sort. Li's new equation could model almost anything, especially the kinds of diverse risk from diverse sources which had previously been unmodelable. It was a magic formula, a magic wand. The CDO and CDS markets were already pretty frisky, but now they went berserk. The CDO market, which was worth $275 million in 2000, grew to $4.7 trillion by 2006. Growth in the CDS market—which had just as much use for the new rocket-science equation—was even more spectacular. By the end of 2001, the CDS markets were worth $920 billion. By the end of 2007, they were worth $62 trillion. That mean that they were everywhere, spread throughout the global financial system, unsupervised and largely invisible even to well-informed investors.

The exciting thing about these new CDOs based on sub-prime mortgages was that they created a world in which everybody won, helped by the central inventions behind the new credit derivatives: securitization and tranching.[1] Banks and financial institutions were now able to buy job lots of mortgages and put them together into a single pool. Then they could divide that pool up into units, which could then be sold to investors. That took the risk off the banks' books and freed the capital to be lent to someone else. If people had been looking at things differently, they would have seen a glaring risk in the fact that the lender—the lender actually at the coal face, the one directly making the loan to the person who wanted a mortgage—now had no need to be particularly bothered about whether or not the borrower could repay. If the borrower defaulted, so what? The lender no longer owned the risk anyway: it had been securitized and sold on. The initial lender was free to quote Bart Simpson: "Sayonara, sucker."

Tranching also played a starring role in the new sub-prime mortgaged-backed CDOs. Remember that tranching is the technique for dividing paying assets into different categories of risk, the safer ones less lucrative, the riskier ones more so. In the case of subprime CDOs, the magic of tranching could be used to create a range of securitized assets, the safest of them being AAA, as safe as U.S. Treasury bills, the safest debt in the world. And then there would be other tranches of debt too, down to the "junk" level—wonderfully, juicily high-yielding debt.

I have several times read explanations of how the CDO geniuses managed to turn poor people who struggled to make their mortgage payments into a source of funds as stable as U.S. Treasury bills. I can understand the explanations with at least part of my brain. The answer was that the cash pouring in went into the equivalent of a series of buckets, the top bucket being the AAA tranche of CDOs, and then, when that was full, spilled over into the AA tranch, then down into the BBB and beyond. If the flow of cash slowed down, well, it would be tough luck on the people holding the lowest buckets, which would be the first to dry up—but then, they were being compensated for that risk by the sexily high yield on the CDOs. The bucket at the top, of course, would never run dry. As long as any money at all was coming in, that bucket would fill up first. That was the idea, and, as I've said, a part of my brain follows the explanation. But a larger part is still left reeling with incredulity at the idea that anyone could be so clever/stupid as to believe that human fallibility could be engineered into nonexistence. They had forgotten Murphy's Law, an important principle of engineering—and not at all the same thing as Sod's Law, which is the facetious idea that the worst thing always happens (in French, *le loi de l'emmerdement maximum*). Murphy's Law is an engineering principle, and it states that if something can go wrong, it will. So the idea that something will go wrong has to be built into a machine—how to monitor it, how to fix it, and what to have in place as a backup when it fails. The designers of the CDOs forgot Murphy's Law. That, to civilians and outsiders, is one of the things which strikes you hardest about this new type of CDOs. You can follow the basic principles of swapping and securitizing debt and stay with the thought that the various inventions were all brought in with the intention of spreading risk and freeing up capital—but there was a point at which people got carried away and the momentum behind this wave of innovative finance went too far.

The designers of the new subprime mortgage-backed CDOs had been given access to the models of risk used by the credit-rating agency Moody's. This was an honorable thing, because companies such as Moody's are at risk of being told that their decisions—their hugely consequential judgments about not just companies but governments—are untransparent and arbitrary. Sunlight is the best disinfectant, and the decision to make the assessment models public was a principled one, but it also gave opportunities for the designers of structured debt—this kind of parceled and chopped-up debt—to custom-create bonds to fit Moody's criteria. That's what the designers of the new CDOs did. There was no limit to the kind of funds that you could have flowing into a CDO; they could even be flows of money from other, preexisting CDOs. Great idea! So people began to design CDOs of CDOs, pools of pools of structured debt, chopped and sliced and then chopped and sliced again, the underlying assets beneath these superingenious financial instruments being people with patchy credit who were struggling to pay back their loans. The new CDOs of CDOs were known as CDO^2, or CDOs squared.

One more component was borrowed from the first of these deals. Remember the SPV, the special purpose vehicle designed to keep the securitized debt off the bank's books (and out of reach of the tax man)? Many of the new CDOs were set up via a similar innovation, the structured investment vehicle, or SIV. These were part-independent subsidiaries of the banks which got some of the earnings from selling off the CDO assets and some from their parent companies, but they did the same thing as the SPVs: they kept assets off the banks' balance sheets and thus helped them avoid the Basel restrictions on capital reserves. The way in which they did that was sheer genius. The Basel rules applied to all credit lines which existed for a year. So the SIVs were set up to last for 364 days or fewer. Magic. The rules existed for a reason, of course—to help keep the banks solvent in times of trouble by keeping the capital levels at a sensibly cautious level—but, really, who gave a damn about that? There's something almost thrilling about the pure indifference to the reasons behind the rules, the reasons why the rules were set up. The banks were certain, absolutely certain, that they knew better. Many of the biggest banks in the world piled into the new mortgage-backed CDOs as if their lives depended on it, among them UBS, RBS, Merrill Lynch, and Citigroup—every one of which has now been bailed out by its respective taxpayers.

It should be stressed that not every financial institution did this. Critics who argue that the bankers are all equally bad—or who argue, as did the U.S. federal judge Richard Posner, that the risks some banks were taking were rational under the circumstances and that the pressures of competition meant that they had no choice—aren't giving sufficient weight to the example of banks which didn't join in.[2] Conspicuous among them was the J.P. Morgan team, which had pretty much invented the entire CDS and CDO industry. They could see how profitable the new mortgage-backed versions of their CDOs were. But after taking a long, hard look at the new business, they took a pass. They simply didn't see how the risks were being engineered down to a safe level. The other banks must be seeing some way of doing it which they couldn't work out. Blythe Masters, the woman in charge of the *Exxon Valdez* deal and of selling the very first BISTRO bonds, and thus one of the creators of the entire CDS industry, was baffled by the CDO boom. "How are the other banks doing it?" she asked. "How are they making so much money?"[3] According to Gillian Tett in *Fool's Gold,* "she was so steeped in the ways of J.P. Morgan that it never occurred to her that the other banks might simply ignore all the risk controls J.P. Morgan had adhered to."

And now the story takes an even nastier turn. If we for a moment recall the idea that money has intentions of its own, we might ask this: what would capital do next? It has found a way of making money at good rates of interest, and it has ingeniously engineered away the associated risks. The only thing which stands in the way of this money-making engine is the shortage of borrowers in the relevant category; because it's important to remember that the underlying source of funds in this amazing new financial invention is still poor or poorish, or unreliable or unreliable-ish, people who are paying back their mortgage loans. They're a specific category: not secure or rich enough to be eligible for ordinary mortgages but not so risky that they won't pay back their loans. As I've already said, mortgage borrowers who default are disastrous for a lender, because each one of them wipes out the gains from a large number of successful loans. It stands to reason that this particular section of the target market, the risky-enough-to-be-profitable, not-risky-enough-to-default subprime borrower, is not going to be infinite in number.

In the days when the mortgage industry rested on a lender looking a borrower in the eye and determining whether to lend her a big chunk of money to be repaid over the next twenty-five years, there would obviously come a moment when credible candidates for such loans could no longer be found. The lender would sigh regretfully, then pack up her papers and shut down new lending. But that model no longer applied. This is where we finally encounter the consequences arising from the fact that the invention of securitization broke banking by separating lender from borrower via selling the loan to somebody else. People wanted to find the money to buy houses, and the money in turn wanted to find a way to get to the people. The result was a huge wave of mortgage-linked financial innovation. So what now happens when the money is looking for new borrowers and the circuit breaker of risk assessment is no longer in place? Answer: the lending goes on regardless. A terrible changeover happens, in which the process of lending no longer is driven by the legitimate desire of poor-but-reliable people to own a house but is instead a manufactured process driven by capital, which is set loose looking for people to sign loans. An epidemic began of what has come to be called "predatory lending": mortgage lenders doing everything they could to sign up borrowers at higher-than-ordinary, subprime interest rates, so that the debt they created could then be pooled and securitized and sold on as tranches of various grades of CDOs. Some of this happened in the United Kingdom, but the overwhelming bulk of activity in this area happened in the United States.

Bear in mind that this was an industry in which a lot of what went on was already of a nature designed if not exactly to stretch the rules, then to look for flexibility within them. That was the whole point. Subprime borrowers were usually people who had poor credit ratings, as calculated by the companies which assess the credit of every single adult, breaking down patterns of spending and credit history to produce a single number. (The three biggest credit ratings agencies in the United States, the ones most relevant to the U.S. subprime story, are Equifax, Experian, and TransUnion; the first two are also the two biggest in the United Kingdom.) In the United States, the number is called the FICO score, after the Fair Isaac Corporation, which invented it, and it runs from 300, meaning you're on the FBI's most-wanted list, to 850, meaning you're Warren Buffett. Actually, having said that, Buffett's credit might not be as high as you'd think, because one of the things which improves your credit is being in debt and having a history of on-time repayments. If Buffett has no mortgage and only one credit card, has his utility bills paid by someone else, and has no outstanding debts or credit lines of any sort, his credit history might conceivably be a little thin. Credit ratings are all about history, and if you don't have much credit in the form of utility bills, credit card bills, and suchlike, your credit history can look sketchy: it's not unknown for people in impeccable financial condition to have poor credit ratings because they don't have enough history of debt. Welcome to Bizarroworld!

I checked my own credit rating with Experian—you can do it online in about two minutes, and if you're worried about identity fraud it's not a bad idea—and was amazed to see that it's pretty good, a point score of 900, which in the British system of scores from 0 to 999 means I'm in the top 30 percent. The reason I'm surprised is that I'm a bit chaotic in my personal affairs and sometimes forget to pay things like utility bills, causing me to be rung up and told off by people from Bangalore as a semiregular event. That hadn't happened recently, however, or my score would have been worse. The credit ratings report and score are all completely explicit and tell you what you need to do to improve your rating and what factors are dragging it down. In my case, the lowering factor is a largish amount of outstanding credit card debt. Most of that is the as-yet-unpaid bill for the MacBook Pro on which I am typing these very words (the same made-in-China one I mentioned last chapter). How postmodern is that? I'm looking up my credit rating on the very laptop which is dragging it down.

Under the American FICO system, 60 percent of scores are in the range from 650 to 799, and the median score—the one with half of all scores below it, and half above it—is 723. From the point of view of the mortgage market, a number over 620 identifies you as a steady-Eddie good citizen, qualifying for one of the "conforming" mortgages sold by Fannie and Freddie. Below that you're in subprime territory, which runs down to about 500, beyond which no one will lend you money for a mortgage. The exact details of the number are hugely important and directly affect both the willingness of lenders to take on a borrower and the amount the borrower will have to pay.

According to Richard Bitner, an expert in the field as the owner of a subprime brokerage and author of a candid and very useful book about the industry, *Confessions of a Subprime Lender: An Insider's Tale of Greed, Fraud, and Ignorance,* subprime borrowers fall into four main categories.[4]

They have a history of being slow to pay; they are under-qualified, because they don't have much credit history (as in the hypothetical Warren Buffett example above); they have had a bad thing happen to them, such as illness or bereavement, which caused them to go off the grid for a time; they're plain unlucky and missed a series of utility payments because they were away and their house sitter forgot to open the envelopes; or they're plain unlucky in another way, because they are on the margin between con-forming and subprime and chose a mortgage broker who, because subprime loans pay more commission, deliberately arranged their application on the wrong side of the sub-prime line.

As that last example shows, the system was chronically, structurally prone to abuse, right from the start. A system designed to bend the rules in the direction of increased flex-ibility and increased lending is always going to be at risk from people who want to use it to cheat and go beyond the rules. Then home prices began to go up, which they did from about 1998, making it more of a stretch for people to buy homes; and then from 2001 credit became dramatically cheaper, making it ever more tempting to make the stretch (especially since prices were going up, making a house look like a bet with lots of upside and no downside); and then new money flooded into the market, money which, because of securitization, didn't actually care about how risky the loans were. Now bear in mind that by 2000 there were 250,000 mortgage brokers in the United States—mortgage brokers being the people who have direct contact with the would-be borrowers and who act as the intermediaries be-tween them and the subprime lenders. The business, in the-ory regulated, was in practice the closest thing imaginable to the Wild West. In Maryland, where I went to look at the effect of foreclosures, individual brokers did not need a license or qualification of any kind. The companies to which they belonged needed licenses, but the individuals needed no credentials. Nationally, there were hundreds of thousands of brokers and millions of new mortgages, all of them beginning with already flexible rules and stretching them as far as they could. It was chaos. The whole idea of "stated income" loans, in which the borrower simply says how much he earns and the lender takes his word for it, is a standing invitation to fraud. These are now known as "liar loans." Their existence led before long to the creation of what is known as the NINJA loan: No Income, No Job or Assets. Why would any sane person lend money to someone with no income, job, or assets? Answer: because they were selling the loan to somebody else, so they didn't care.

Bitner left the business in 2005, after a moment of clarity with a mortgage application. He had clients named the Cutters, who bought a house in 2005 but quickly fell behind on payments when Margaret Cutter became ill. She lost her job and had no health insurance; a cruel double whammy meaning that her costs rocketed upward just as her income crashed. Bitner ran through their options and explained that their best one was to accept that they couldn't pay the loan and give up their house. They accepted that, and their home was repossessed. But it was when he went through the file afterward that the penny dropped. The Cutters had borrowed $90,000 on a joint income of $2,800 a month. After putting down their deposit of $4,500, they had $250 left in the bank—that was the sum total of all their assets. After the mortgage payments, they had $700 left for all expenses each month. They had a lousy credit rating and a poor history of repaying debt. There was no evidence that they had ever paid rent to anyone. In the last three years, neither of them had been employed for more than nine months at a stretch. And—this is the real sting—*all of that was fine.* In Bitner's words, "we did nothing wrong." The Cutters met all the relevant criteria for this kind of loan. It was by the book; the subprime book. And that was what caused Bitner to decide that it was time to walk away.

The only thing unusual about that story is that Bitner felt ill about what was going on, quit, and wrote a book about it. In Baltimore I heard many variations of the same tale, featuring loans which should never have been made to people who would never have been able to pay them back and shading into darker practices. "We all saw it coming, but nobody would listen," Mary Waldrow of the Belair-Edison Community Association told me. "A lot of people in [the Maryland housing coalition] saw it coming." Belair-Edison is a poor East Baltimore neighborhood which has had a third of its homes foreclosed on over the last decade—and when you hear what the lenders got up to and the extent to which they depended on the desperation and naiveté of first-generation home owners, it's no surprise. The city of Baltimore is currently suing one of the banks involved in extending loans, Wells Fargo, on the basis that it systematically targeted African Americans to be put on subprime loans, even when the borrower qualified for a better rate. The case is ongoing, but affidavits already entered into the record report that, in the words of one former employee of the bank, "Wells Fargo mortgage had an emerging-markets unit that specifically targeted black churches, because it figured church leaders had a lot of influence and could convince congregants to take out subprime loans."[5]

The whole market was riddled with scams and tricks. One standard move: a buyer finds a property, fixes up a loan with a mortgage broker, and arrives at the settlement hearing, where the deal is to be done and the papers are signed. When there is an attorney present at the hearing—which there doesn't have to be under Maryland law—the attorney is representing the company holding the title deeds, not the purchaser. At the settlement, the mortgage broker says, "Ah, shucks, I know we said we could get you a loan at 6 percent but unfortunately we couldn't, the rate here is 12 percent, but don't worry, if you sign now we can change it later." But that's not true. You can't change it later. In the words of Phillip Robinson of the Civil Justice Network, a nonprofit leading the charge in the legal battle against foreclosures, "That's a common scam. 'Just sign and we'll fix it tomorrow.' They promise six or eight percent. Then they come to the table and they offer a different rate. Another thing you can sign with these documents is, you waive your right to a jury trial, go to private arbitration. Do they ever explain that to you? No. There's another document they make you sign that says, 'You have a right to receive a copy of the appraisal for your property, but only if you ask for it in writing and then we have ninety days to give it to you.' Well if you get that ninety days after settlement, what good is that appraisal to you? The appraisal that you already paid for? You need to see that appraisal to know that the house is worth what you're borrowing. Also, even when you do see it, the appraisals use comparisons from blocks away and two years old—they're worthless."

And the shocking thing—or at least, the shocking thing to me, because everyone in the field has got used to it—is that this is perfectly legal. It's all legit. The principle is that of caveat emptor: the mortgage brokers are salesmen, and if you buy something from a salesman, the onus is on you to not get screwed.

In response to this, Phillip Robinson and his colleagues at Civil Justice have come up with an idea which is both noble in its motivations and devastatingly, dazzlingly, breathtakingly cynical. This is the idea: how do you drive change in America? Real, noncosmetic change? Answer: by finding ways for lawyers to make money. "We do litigation that no one else will do, we try to teach the private bar how to do it once we've figured out how to do it success-fully," Robinson explains. "Our theory is, if you can get the private bar to help home owners with these predatory real estate practices, then we can begin to drive change. We've done that pretty successfully for ten or eleven years." So Robinson's idea is to locate a category of mortgage fraud so flagrant, and so clear in the evidentiary record, that even courts not minded to rule against Wall Street will find for his client. Then he will have a template that he can teach to private law firms, and they will start to file cases and win proper money. "My hook is, if you can show someone how to make money, a private attorney can do the same kind of case a hundred times." And then, because by this point it will be costing the banks real money, the banks will finally begin to change their practices.

The particular type of case Robinson is working on now is a scam called foreclosure rescue. All over the blighted parts of Baltimore I had seen signs with wording based on the theme "Home at risk? Call us!" I felt a small flicker of hope: perhaps someone had the best interests of East Balti-more's vulnerable neighborhoods at heart after all; perhaps their plight wasn't so bad . . . I should have known better. Those ads are touting a complex scam: the scammers offer the endangered foreclosee a way out of her plight by sign-ing over the deeds of her house to someone with good credit, who takes out a new mortgage on the property. The idea is that the original home owner has a year to fix her credit and save up some money, and then she can take back her home. In the meantime, the "rescuer" charges the original home owner a string of fees, all of them notionally helping her rebuild her credit but in practice simply running down the victim's bank balance and stripping her assets. The usual technique is for these fees and charges to go unmentioned when the home owner is being enticed into the deal; then, when she turns up at the settlement meeting, she is presented with dozens of pieces of paper to sign, without warning and without legal representation. Some of these pieces of paper assign fees to the mortgage rescuer. Most of the time, the person with good credit is a straw entity, not even a knowing party to the transaction, so none of the mortgage money is ever repaid. The first the home owner knows about this is when the bank slaps a foreclosure notice on the house, and bang, she's lost her home. Now, the point of legal interest is to do with how much care the bank should take in extending a loan to the straw person. At what point does it have to interest itself in the fact that the whole thing is a scam? At what point does it have to bestir itself to think about the home owner's interests?

I say "her" because in the test case Robinson is currently pursuing, the woman who lost her home is Harriette Julian, who entered into one of these foreclosure rescue agreements with a local company. She signed the deeds of her house over to Lashawn Wilson—who wasn't present at the settlement meeting and was represented only by a purported signature on a piece of paper. The idea was that Ms. Julian would rebuild her credit and then, after a period of time, buy back her house. Everyone was aware that Ms. Julian was in foreclosure. Ms. Wilson was buying the house for $482,000 but had no income. Not only a little income: no income. That was a routine feature of these scams. So these are the things the bank ignored: One, Ms. Wilson's HUD-1 (a standard form used to itemize transaction fees) had no address. Two, foreclosure scams were known to be everywhere: a new Maryland law, the Protection of Home-owners in Foreclosure Act, had been passed specifically targeting them. Three, Harriette Julian wasn't moving from the home she was signing away: another classic sign of a foreclosure scam. Four, no payments were made on the mortgage, not one, ever: yet another classic sign. Five, during the process, Harriette Julian and Lashawn Wilson told the bank that they were the victim of a foreclosure scam— but the bank ignored all of that and, having gone ahead with the loan, then went ahead with the foreclosure. Civil Justice and Phillip Robinson are trying to show that at some point in the process, the onus falls on the bank to actually give a shit—and thereby create a way for lawyers to make money out of it. At which point, the bank will have to start acting as if it gives a shit.

"Most of my clients who are in foreclosure," Robinson said to me, "they're hardworking, they're making money, but they couldn't afford the loan from the beginning. Remember *It's a Wonderful Life*? It's not like that any more. They don't care about you. If they did, they wouldn't give you a $300,000 loan if you didn't have a job and had no chance of paying it back."

From 2005 onward, across the industry, most of the lending was reckless and some of it actively criminal. Bitner's estimate at the time he left the business was that 70 percent of mortgage applications were erroneous or fraudulent; and that was before the very worst of the excesses. As for what the worst of it was, well, that would be deliberate fraud, of which there was much, starting with lies about employment and income. A survey from 2007 found that by 2006, 60 percent of subprime applicants were lying about their income by more than 50 percent—so more than half of applicants were lying by exaggerating their income by more than half.[6] By that point, more than half of all applications for mortgages were either "piggyback" loans, meaning that they were double loans taken out to buy the same property, or "liar loans," in which applicants were invited to state their own income, or "no doc" loans, in which the borrower produced no paperwork. Gee, what could possibly go wrong? And all this was just business as usual, legitimate lending, not allowing for instances in which there was systematic, organized fraud involving false identities and multiple applications for credit. The whole business was set up to lend, no questions asked—no real questions asked, anyway. The loans generated money for everyone and huge amounts of subprime debt so that the banking industry could create all the CDOs it wanted. And as for the idea that those people's mortgage payments were being miraculously transmuted into AAA-grade investments . . .

FIVE

THE MISTAKE

And yet the financial industry could still have got away with it. All the things described up until now could have been survived, and the resulting chaos avoided, if it hadn't been for a single mistake. It was the mistake which underpinned all the other mistakes and errors of judgment; it was the mistake which took the global economic system up to the edge of the abyss, and although in some senses it was not a single mistake, because it was made by lots of people in lots of different places on many varied occasions, in another way it was the same mistake everywhere. That mistake can be summed up in a single word: risk. The bankers made inaccurate calculations about the mathematics of risk. That in essence was the mistake which destroyed some banks, forced others into public ownership, put taxpayers on the hook for hundreds of billions of dollars, and brought the world financial system to a juddering, panicky standstill. It led directly to the slowdown currently dominating every economy in the world.

I'm willing to make a bet. This is it: that somewhere

near you, wherever and whoever you are, there is a killer. A killer you've never noticed as a killer; a killer you've never thought about as a real danger to you. I'm not talking about an invisible killer, like a virus or bacteria; I'm not talking about an obvious killer, like the idiot in the 4×4 roaring down the road outside or the mugger lurking by the broken streetlight, I'm talking about a killer who is plainly visible, whom you see every day, whom you've known your whole life, and to whom you never give a second's thought. This killer kills more than a thousand men and women in the United Kingdom every year, year in and year out, yet you've never heard a word about the dangers it represents. Bear in mind that cars and road accidents—that's drivers, passengers, pedestrians, cyclists, everybody—come to a total of less than 3,000 deaths a year. This killer is between a third and a half as dangerous as all the road traffic in the United Kingdom.

Give up? I'm talking about stairs. That's right, humanity's friend the humble stair. If stairs were invented today and a full analysis of their dangers were made, along with the gory statistics—the literally gory statistics—there would be an impassioned, sustained, and I'm pretty sure eventually successful campaign to have them banned on health and safety grounds. It's happened to much safer things than stairs. Stairs are absolutely lethal. I even myself know someone killed by his own stairs, one of the 1,000-plus deaths in a typical year.* Yet we don't perceive stairs as being risky.

---

* Although 21,648 Americans were killed by falls last year, you can't tell how many were killed by stairs because the various types of falls are not separated out in the official mortality statistics. Perhaps the feared stairs lobby has been at work suppressing the dark truth. In the United Kingdom, the government's mortality statistics for 2007 list only 620 deaths-by-stairs, perhaps because the injuries sustained falling down stairs often

They're filed away in the part of our consciousness where daily objects live, not in the part which attends to dangers and threats and risks to life. We don't see these things entirely rationally, and familiarity breeds not contempt but a lack of attention. Why? We don't really know. Our intuitive understanding of risks and of numbers is limited. The explanations usually reached for are of the currently fashionable cod-evolutionary-psychology sort which reaches back to ancestral humanity on the African savanna. We are bad with risk because our hunter-gatherer ancestors blah blah blah. The long and the short of it is that we aren't all that good with risk.

In fact, we aren't all that good with numbers in general. We seem to be hardwired to make certain sorts of mathematical mistakes. This is a profound challenge to the way much of the economics profession sees the world. It would be such a powerful explanatory tool if it were to turn out that we always act, from an economic point of view, rationally. If you plug assumptions of economic rationality into your view of the world, you can come up with all sorts of fascinating explanations of everything from why there are so many teenage single mothers (they were making a rational choice to marry the state), why the bankers got every-

---

take a little while to finish the victim off. The government acknowledged the figure of a thousand deaths a year with a stair-awareness campaign in 2000. The victims are overwhelmingly older people: only seventy Britons under the age of forty-five were killed by stairs. A warning about government mortality statistics: if you are of a nervous or hypochondriacal disposition, avoid them at all costs. Here are some of the categories of deaths: "Accidental suffocation or strangling in bed" (eight deaths), "Contact with plant thorns and spikes and sharp leaves" (one death), and "Drowning and submersion while in bathtub" (eighteen deaths). Interestingly, only one person died after being bitten by a rat but ten from being "bitten or struck by other mammals." But which mammals? Dogs? If so, why not say so? Badgers? Dolphins?

thing so wrong in the run-up to the credit crunch (they
were responding rationally to a skewed balance of risks
and rewards), and why the Dutch tulip bubble took place
(it was a rational application of greater fool theory). Most
of this exemplifies what I would argue is the most common
mistake of very smart people: the assumption that other
people's minds work in the same way that theirs do. To
noneconomists, the mathematically based models and assumptions of rational conduct which permeate the field often have the appearance, at best, of toys, entertaining but
by definition of limited utility; at worst, they can seem willful delusions, determinedly ignoring reality. The general
reader needs no persuading about the influence of non-
rational, noneconomic forces on economic thinking. The
economics profession, however, is split between economic
rationalists in the Milton Friedman tradition and economic
liberals in the tradition of John Maynard Keynes, and the
subject of strict rationality is the occasion of a permanent
pitched battle. The fact that noneconomists see the general
assumption of rationality as self-evidently ridiculous has no
effect on economists. What has had an effect, however, is
the work of two Israeli psychologist-economists, Daniel
Kahneman and Amos Tversky, who have produced a body
of work studying "the susceptibility to erroneous intuitions
of intelligent, sophisticated, and perceptive individuals,"
in the words of the fascinating autobiography written by
Kahneman on the occasion of winning the Nobel Prize in
2002.

I have a confession to make about Kahneman and Tversky. I'd never heard of them until Kahneman won the
Nobel,* and when I first read about their work, it seemed

----

* Tversky would have won it too if it hadn't been for his too early death
in 1996. The prize is actually the Sveriges Riksbank Bank Prize in Eco-

to me to consist of things which were surprising only to economists. One of their interests was "hindsight bias," the way in which a random sequence of events is given structure and narrative by the false perspective of looking back over it from its outcome. Another was "loss aversion," the fact that people place a higher value on not losing money than on gaining it; another was on "the law of small numbers," referring to people's tendency to draw overconfident conclusions from small amounts of evidence. Their particular interest was in "heuristics," the patterns of thinking people use to interpret data, and the strong conclusion they reached was that people's heuristics are often wrong; we are much less accurate and less rational in our thinking than we believe ourselves to be. My initial reaction to this was to think, so what: everybody except economists knows this anyway.

Then I had a look at their work firsthand and soon came to realize that I was missing the point. Kahneman and Tversky directly take on the central shibboleth of contemporary academic economics. The assumption of rationality permeates modern economics and is one of the reasons the field has sharply contracted in its practical usefulness. Instead of being concerned with what actually happens in practice—this is left to a subfield within microeconomics, which is, broadly speaking, the study of people's behavior and decision making—the field is increasingly preoccupied with developing pseudomathematical formulae. These provide models of behavior which never quite fit what actually happens, in a way which resembles the physical sciences gone wrong: instead of equations describing reality, economics

---

nomic Sciences in Memory of Alfred Nobel—people refer to it as the Nobel Prize in Economics, but strictly speaking it isn't a Nobel Prize since it wasn't one of the five prizes Nobel himself set up: Physiology or Medicine, Chemistry, Physics, Literature, and Peace.

produces equations describing ideal conditions and theoretical clarity of a type which never occurs in practice. Many disciplines suffer badly from envy of the physical sciences, of a world in which $f = mv$ means exactly what it says; academic economics has a particularly bad case of physics envy. Assumptions of rationally modeled behavior are a big part of this wrong turn in the field, and that is why Kahneman and Tversky's work is so important: because it proves—not asserts, *proves*—the ways in which our thinking, our heuristics, have built-in mistakes. This, from the point of view of the economists' received wisdom, is revolutionary. The impact of their work on economics has been big and is only going to get bigger (and it's readable, too, which is not something you can often say about academic economics).

Kahneman tells three great stories in his official Nobel biography (even that is unusually readable and interesting), the first about how he became interested in psychology while living as a small child of about eight under the Nazi occupation of France:

In one experience I remember vividly, there was a rich range of shades. It must have been late 1941 or early 1942. Jews were required to wear the Star of David and to obey a 6 p.m. curfew. I had gone to play with a Christian friend and had stayed too late. I turned my brown sweater inside out to walk the few blocks home. As I was walking down an empty street, I saw a German soldier approaching. He was wearing the black uniform that I had been told to fear more than others—the one worn by specially recruited SS soldiers. As I came closer to him, trying to walk fast, I noticed that he was looking at me intently. Then he beckoned me over, picked me up, and hugged me. I was terrified that he would notice the star inside my sweater. He was speaking to me with great emotion, in German. When he put me down, he opened his wallet, showed me a picture of a boy, and gave me some money. I went home more certain than ever that my mother was right: people were endlessly complicated and interesting.[1]

The next story came from Kahneman's time in the Israeli army, where he devised the questionnaire used to test recruits' suitability for various kind of operations. The need to do this came from his encounter with existing methods, which, in his view, simply didn't work:

> We used methods that had been developed by the British Army in the Second World War. One test involved a leaderless group challenge, in which eight candidates, with all insignia of rank removed and only numbers to identify them, were asked to lift a telephone pole from the ground and were then led to an obstacle, such as a 2.5-meter wall, where they were told to get to the other side of the wall without the pole touching either the ground or the wall, and without any of them touching the wall.* If one of these things happened, they had to declare it and start again.
> Two of us would watch the exercise, which often took half an hour or more. We were looking for manifestations of the candidates' characters, and we

---

* As far as I know, the British army's officer selection process still uses a version of this test.

saw plenty: true leaders, loyal followers, empty
boasters, wimps—there were all kinds. Under the
stress of the event, we felt, the soldiers' true nature
would reveal itself, and we would be able to tell who
would be a good leader and who would not. But the
trouble was that, in fact, we could not tell. Every
month or so we had a "statistics day," during which
we would get feedback from the officer-training
school, indicating the accuracy of our ratings of candidates' potential. The story was always the same:
our ability to predict performance at the school was
negligible. But the next day, there would be another
batch of candidates to be taken to the obstacle field,
where we would face them with the wall and see
their true natures revealed. I was so impressed by the
complete lack of connection between the statistical
information and the compelling experience of insight
that I coined a term for it: "the illusion of validity."

And then a final, shaping experience came in 1958 at
the Austen Riggs Center in Stockbridge, Massachusetts, a
psychoanalytical center. There was a weekly case conference on Friday.

Those attending would have received and read,
the night before, a folder with detailed notes from
every department about the person in question.
There would be a lively exchange of impressions
among the staff, which included the fabled Erik
Erikson. Then the patient would come in for a group
interview, which was followed by a brilliant discussion. On one of those Fridays, the meeting took
place and was conducted as usual, despite the fact
that the patient had committed suicide during the

night. It was a remarkably honest and open discussion, marked by the contradiction between the powerful retrospective sense of the inevitability of the event and the obvious fact that the event had not been foreseen. This was another cognitive illusion to be understood.

The study of these "cognitive illusions" and the effect of Kahneman and Tversky's work will resonate for many years to come, because it forces economists to acknowledge the ways in which human beings don't and perhaps can't make accurate assessments of perceptions and probabilities. One simple and now-famous-to-economists example: people will judge the probability of a deadly flood in North America to be lower than that of a deadly flood in California. Naming the specific place—with, perhaps, subliminal associations of earthquakes and fires—triggers something in the brain which makes disaster seem more likely. Another famous example, not from Kahneman and Tversky but similar to their work in its gist: if a test for some disease is 95 percent accurate and the disease affects one person in a thousand, and you go for a test and it comes back positive, what's the probability that you have the disease? Most respondents say, well, the test is accurate, so the probability is 95 percent. The correct answer is 2 percent, because if you test 1,000 people, the test will give 50 positives, whereas only one of the population actually has the illness. But the real sting in the story is the fact that this was the answer given to the question not by members of the public but by doctors. Our hardwired difficulties with probability and risk go very deep.[2]

Kahneman and his colleagues have created a hugely important body of work with a single big takeaway for the nonexpert reader: they have proved that we humans, even expert humans, are chronically prone to make certain sorts of cognitive mistakes. We have a particular propensity to errors in relation to risk. Given that, it was perhaps not surprising that it was a mistake involving risk that lay behind the credit crunch. It was that which Alan Greenspan was talking about when he appeared before the U.S. Congress's House Committee on Oversight and Government Reform on October 23, 2008, and spoke about "a once-in-a-century credit tsunami" based on a "whole intellectual edifice" which had now collapsed. That's an amazing admission for Greenspan to have made, given that he more than anyone else was in charge of the monetary policies behind both the long boom and the abrupt bust. He had charge of the Federal Reserve under four presidents, from Ronald Reagan, who appointed him in 1987, to the second President Bush, whom he served until his retirement in 2006, and during that time he oversaw the response to several crises, from the crash of October 1987 (during which share prices fell 20 percent in a single day) through the recession of 1991, the implosion of LTCM in 1998, and the dot-com bust of 2001. For most of this time, Greenspan's militant advocacy of deregulation and laissez-faire capitalism seemed to be an effective intellectual underpinning of his policies. Greenspan was a close friend and disciple of Ayn Rand, the Russian-born philosopher who advocated a philosophy she called "Objectivism" (she wanted to call it "Existentialism," but some pesky Euros had already bagged that name).* Objectivism is undergoing a vogue on the Internet at the moment, perhaps because its libertarian ideol-

---

*Rand was also a huge fan of *Charlie's Angels*. "It's the only romantic television show today. It's not realistic. It's not about the gutter, it's not about the half-wit retarded children and all the other kind of shows today. It's about three attractive girls doing impossible things, and because

ogy appeals to a certain type of computer nerd. Rand's central ideas focused on her belief that society must get out of the way of great men. Man is "a heroic being, with his own happiness as the moral purpose of his life," and the only good society is capitalism, which Rand glossed as follows: "When I say 'capitalism,' I mean a full, pure, uncontrolled, unregulated laissez-faire capitalism."[3] Today Objectivism seems a sophomoric belief system, whose main truth lies in its unexpressed but profound longing for the world to be a much simpler place than it is. Still, there's no denying Objectivism's impact on the world, thanks to its direct influence on the most economically powerful man alive, Alan Greenspan. His emphasis throughout all his years in office was on the belief—the mystical belief—that markets could be entirely trusted to regulate themselves. That was why it was such an explosive admission when Greenspan went before the House committee and said, "Those of us who have looked to the self-interest of lending institutions to protect shareholders' equity (myself especially) are in a state of shocked disbelief." In response to questioning, he said that he had found "a flaw in the model that I perceived is the critical functioning structure that defines how the world works."[4]

It's worth dwelling on that phrase: "the critical functioning structure that defines how the world works." That's a hell of a big thing for a man like Greenspan to find a flaw in. That flaw was to do with risk. To understand what happened, we have first to get a grip on the financial understanding of risk.

Moneymen don't see risk in the same way that civilians

they're impossible, that's what makes it interesting." This is from a Phil Donahue interview available online. It even sounds better in her accent.

do. To most of us, risk is for the most part a bad thing; at best, it's something we seek out under specific circumstances to generate a feeling that things are just dangerous enough to be exciting. In the world of money, risk is different: it's desirable. That's because in investments, risks are correlated with rewards. You can invest your money entirely risk free: all you do is buy a U.S. Treasury bill and hold it to maturity, and you will know, for sure, exactly what your return will be. Note that buying bonds with a view to trading them—selling them if the price goes up—is not risk free, because the price of the bond can go down. It's also the case that inflation can overtake the interest rate paid by the bond and you could end up making a net loss in inflation-adjusted terms. From both those points of view, it's apparent that something being risk free can nonetheless involve you losing some money. But the fact remains, if you buy a T-bill and hold it to maturity, you get exactly what you paid for, guaranteed.

So why not do that? Well, at the time of writing, a T-bill that you hold for a year will yield 0.41 percent. You pay quite a high price for complete safety. Historically, the rate of completely risk-free investment, taking out the effect of inflation, has been about 3 percent. Three percent isn't nothing; in twenty-four years time, 3 percent compounded will double your money, which isn't bad going for no risk at all. On the other hand, 6 percent will double your money in twelve years, and 12 percent will double your money in six; so if you invest $10,000 at 3 percent, a quarter of a century later you'll have $20,000, whereas your more aggressive chum who invests it at 12 percent will have $160,000. Compound interest, plus increased risk, is a powerful formula for making a lot more money than you can make in complete safety.

For this reason, the world of money is all about risk: seeking it and seeking to master it, to understand the risks being taken and to adjust one's thinking accordingly. A borrower will always try to get the lowest possible rate for his loan, and a lender will always try to get the highest, and the perennially shifting dance between them is determined by the balance of risk, a constantly moving assessment of risk and probability which gives a role to all sort of factors to do with external circumstances, business conditions, interest rates, actuarial tables, and many phenomena which are ultimately to do with mood—with what Keynes called "animal spirits." * The dance between lenders and borrowers—a cross between a dance and a fight, like capoeira perhaps—doesn't always lead to accurate prices for risk, because over time one side can do much better than the other at the agreed rate; but it does lead to prices which perfectly summarize the balance of views about risk at any given moment. My mortgage loan cost me 7.25 percent when it was taken out; that price represented the sum of, on the one hand, what the mortgage market thought of the risk it was taking in lending to me and the most cash it could squeeze out of me, and, on the other hand, from my point of view, the cheapest access to capital I could find at the time. (Just to show how the bal-

---

* In fact, Keynes seemed to use the term to refer to the basic optimistic will to act which underlies much investment. "Most, probably, of our decisions to do something positive, the full consequences of which will be drawn out over many days to come, can only be taken as the result of animal spirits—a spontaneous urge to action rather than inaction, and not as the outcome of a weighted average of quantitative benefits multiplied by quantitative probabilities." In their book *Animal Spirits*, George Akerlof and Robert Shiller appropriated the term to apply to the whole area of emotion and confidence in economics, and it's in that spirit that I'm using the term here.

ance of these things changes, I thought that the interest rate was a bit higher than I'd like when I took out the mortgage. But now I'm a lot happier than the bank is, because it was an adjustable-rate mortgage and is currently costing me 1 percent. For an ordinary citizen, capital doesn't come much cheaper than that. In fact, Woolwich/Barclays no longer issues this particular kind of mortgage. So although I was comprehensively screwed on my first endowment mortgage two decades ago, I have very, very slightly screwed— perhaps one-eighth screwed—the bank this time. That's an example of how although the market gives a very good summary of how risks look at any particular moment, the balance will change over time, and one side is likely to come out ahead.) The thing to understand in the financial world is that people actively go looking for risk, because a riskier investment will be a higher-yielding investment. Then they try to master the risk. If you ever come across an investment which is less risky but yields more, take it. You have found the Philosopher's Stone.

How does the industry seek to master the risks? Through mathematics. The commonsense version of what sophisticated investors do is diversification, a technique so old it's mentioned in the Talmud, where the strategy advocated is to have a third of your assets in trade, a third in cash, and a third in land. Here's a nice simple example of diversification from Wikipedia:

"On a particular island the entire economy consists of two companies: one that sells umbrellas and another that sells sunscreen. If a portfolio is completely invested in the company that sells umbrellas, it will have strong performance during the rainy season but poor performance when the weather is sunny. The reverse occurs if the portfolio is invested only in the sunscreen company, the alternative investment: the portfolio will be high performance when the sun is out but will tank when clouds roll in. To minimize the weather-dependent risk in the example portfolio, the investment should be split between the companies. With this diversified portfolio, returns are decent no matter the weather, rather than alternating between excellent and terrible."

What the pros do is a sophisticated version of that.[5] I've mentioned Myron Scholes and Fischer Black's 1973 paper as the moment when the derivatives market underwent its modernist revolution. In share investing, the equivalent moment was the 1952 publication in the *Journal of Finance* of a paper called "Portfolio Selection" by Harry Markowitz, a twenty-five-year-old graduate student at the University of Chicago. Markowitz had read Hume while still in high school: "I was particularly struck by David Hume's argument that, though we release a ball a thousand times, and each time, it falls to the floor, we do not have a necessary proof that it will fall the thousand-and-first time." By the time he was at the university, this had translated into an interest in uncertainty, and when Markowitz began to study for his Ph.D. on the mathematics of share pricing, he was hit by an idea. The current theory of share prices, the "fair-value" theory of John Burr Williams, argued that the present value of a share was no more than the value of the future dividends it would make, discounted to allow for the effect of inflation. Williams, in other words, disagreed with the various thinkers who stressed the casino-like aspect of share investing in favor of a belief that shares did in fact have an intrinsic, measurable value. Markowitz, working on his Ph.D., fell to reflecting on the fact that the fair-value theory made no allowance for uncertainty; for the fact that, in reality, we can have no sure idea what dividends a share will pay in the future. Because of that, investors diversify their portfolios, as in the umbrellas-and-sunscreen example, and Markowitz began to study the mathematics of how they diversify and how the movement of different shares in different directions could be studied and used to reduce the overall risk of a portfolio of shares.

Markowitz's ideas boiled down to two fundamental insights. The first was about volatility. We all know that the main thing about a share price is how much it goes up or down over time. That much was obvious. But Markowitz saw another thing: that as well as knowing how much a share went up, it was also essential to know how much it wobbled up and down en route to its destination. That was critical, because it told you how much risk you were taking on. A share that over time made an average gain of 5 percent a year but in any given year stood a good chance of losing a quarter of its value was a very different proposition from a share which made the same gain but hardly ever lost more than 10 percent. The owner of the less volatile share will sleep much better, for a start. So now there were two principal numbers for a share, the average growth and the average volatility; both numbers, taken together, gave the investor dramatically more information than just the growth on its own.

Another idea gave the first even more power. It was to do with correlation, which is the way in which shares either do or don't move together. In our umbrellas-and-sunscreen example, the share prices of the companies have a negative correlation: when one goes up, the other goes down. It's easy to think of other real-world examples: shares in online gambling companies versus shares in casinos, say, or (more subtly) shares in oil companies versus shares in car manufacturers (because high oil prices will mean people buy fewer cars). Some of the correlations are between whole sectors of stocks with, for instance, technology shares having a low correlation with service industry stocks (meaning they tend to move in opposite directions) and real estate having an even lower correlation with oil services (Why? No idea). Again, correlation is something that can be measured, using historic data, and given a precise number: the math tells you just how much specific shares have historically been correlated with each other.

Markowitz showed how important volatility plus correlation can be as a tool in managing a portfolio of investments. By identifying stocks which don't move in the same direction, investors can get the upside of share price movements while significantly reducing the up-and-down volatility of the overall portfolio. In his history of risk, *Against the Gods: The Remarkable Story of Risk,* Peter Bernstein makes the point with a chart showing a portfolio of investments in thirteen emerging stock markets. Over the two-and-a-half-year period of the chart, the portfolio of a little bit of everything grew at just under 2 percent a month—a tasty yield for any portfolio in any language—and had less volatility than any single one of its thirteen constituent markets. Since some of those markets had a 20 percent chance of moving by a third in any given month, the stability given by the use of negative correlation would be invaluable in preventing the investor from going nuts with anxiety. All this led to the invention of what came to be called the "efficient" portfolio, one which maximized the possible return for any chosen level of risk; basically, an efficient portfolio is one which uses volatility and correlation to engineer away unnecessary risks.

Notice, however, that a small sideways shuffle has taken place. When you and I and the postman talk about risk, we are talking about the possibility of something bad happening—of being bitten by a dog, say, or catching swine flu. When financial types talk about risk, they are usually— as in the examples above—talking about volatility. Volatility is the measure of how much prices seesaw around, which isn't at all what the rest of us mean by risk, not least because volatility embraces both upward movement, which is what we want from shares, and downward movement, which is what we don't. So risk in the mathematical sense is both a good thing and a bad thing. This is confusing. Don't worry if you feel confused, because you're in good company. Warren Buffett insists on the old-school, com- monsense understanding of risk and sticks to his own view that "risk comes from not knowing what you're doing." That, as the current crisis has shown, is no more than the plain truth; but it's also a philosophical position directly at odds with the current trend in banking.

The new approach to risk was one of the things which put mathematicians at the heart of modern banking. One new invention in particular put them there. The new model was first adopted by the U.S. company Bankers Trust in the late 1970s, under the chairmanship of Charles Sanford. In his view, "successful people understand that risk, properly conceived, is often highly productive rather than something to avoid. They appreciate that risk is an advantage to be used rather than a pitfall to be skirted. Such people under- stand that taking calculated risks is quite different from be- ing rash."[6] He put this into practice by encouraging Bankers Trust to develop a precisely quantified measure of risk, a system which became known as risk-adjusted return on capital, or RAROC. RAROC offered a numerical analy- sis of risk and added to it a measure of the impact of that risk on a business's profitability; just as portfolio management provided a way of assessing and optimizing the risk of a set of share holdings, RAROC did the same for a company's or bank's range of businesses. In time, however, the industry came to prefer a newer model of risk, called value at risk, or VAR. This was a statistical technique which really took off in the later 1980s, as a response to the Black Monday stock market crash of October 1987. On that occasion, many players were appalled by the speed and severity of their losses—losses which, it's now thought, were in large part caused by computer programs running "portfolio insurance." That was yet another invention, the brainchild of a young California academic named Hayne Leland, who worked out that thanks to the Black-Scholes equation and subsequent takeoff of the options industry, options could now be used to create a form of insurance against share prices dropping, not just one by one but across an entire investment portfolio.

Leland had his idea in 1976; by 1987, the use of portfolio insurance was widespread. There was a problem, though: the most commonly used form of insurance was against the whole index of the top 500 shares, the S&P 500. People insured their holdings against a basket of all 500 top stocks. The idea was that if prices started to go down beyond a certain point, the computer program would kick in and sell the stocks, thus preventing further losses. That way, there was insurance guaranteeing that investors would never lose more than a predetermined amount of money. The problem was that everybody's automatic program was set up the same way, and all the progams concentrated on selling a basket of the top 500 stocks. This was an accident waiting to happen, and it duly happened on Monday, October 19, 1987. Stocks had been wobbling downward as investors' nerves grew unsteady. Over the previous weekend, a number of sell orders had built up. This meant that the market, when it opened on the Monday, started falling as the sell orders were executed; the portfolio insurance kicked in and began automatically selling shares. But because everyone's automatic programs were kicking in at the same time and trying to sell the same basket of stocks, no buyers could be found, so the stocks dropped more and the automatic selling programs kept on trying to sell into a market with no buyers. The result was that the Dow Jones Industrial Average dropped 22.6 percent in one day, worse than anything that had happened in the great Crash of 1929.

That left many bankers saying, Never again. In retrospect, Black Monday looks more like a speed bump in the general upward movement of markets from 1982; nonetheless, it also showed how the increasingly interlinked nature of markets and computer-assisted trading could make bad things happen with great speed. Black Monday came out of the blue and cost a lot of people a lot of money. It left them wanting to know just what risks they were running at any given moment. It had started to become obvious that now that financial institutions were so big and complicated, different parts of the same firm would, without realizing it, be making very similar bets, thus unwittingly magnifying certain risks. VAR was the statistical tool which promised to let managers get a grip on this. It was first adopted by Dennis Weatherstone, the CEO of J.P. Morgan. In 1989, he initiated something called the 4:15 report, a piece of paper which landed on his desk every day at 4:15 p.m., a quarter of an hour after the markets closed, carrying a VAR number which summed up the risk the bank was taking that day. VAR has three components: a time frame, usually in the one-day to two-week range; a number stating the amount of money at risk; and a fixed probability, usually either 1 or 5 percent, expressing the chance that that money will be lost. So you might have a VAR of one day, $1,000,000, and 5 percent. That means that there is a 5 percent chance that you will lose $1,000,000 within the next twenty-four hours. Put more cheerfully, there is a 95 percent chance that you won't lose $1,000,000. The way to think of VAR is as a worst-case scenario, a statement of how much you can lose within—that is the hugely important proviso, *within*—the given range of probabilities. Outside that range, all bets are off. This is a vital fact, and one of the dangers with VAR is that, in the dialogue between the quants and the managers, the meaning of the figures can be mislaid. The percentage sets the "VAR break," as it's called, the point at which all bets are off and you can lose not just your shirt but your house.

It was easy, though, for people to hear a VAR of one day, 1 percent, and $1,000,000 as telling them that the worst that could happen was that they would lose a million bucks—which wasn't what the figures were telling them, not at all. (And by the way, that one-per-cent-per-day outcome is still likely to happen a couple of times a year.) Still, VAR brought a degree of certainty where none had previously existed, and that alone felt like a breakthrough. The increasing prevalence of derivatives in the financial system also added to the popularity of VAR, because it provided a way for managers (and investors, regulators, and everybody else) who didn't understand derivatives to put a figure on the risks that were being run. In 1997, the U.S. Securities and Exchange Commission required corporations fooling around with derivatives to give quantitative statements of their activities; lots of firms chose to do so by publishing VAR figures. VAR became the industry standard, so much

so that it was used as the preferred measure of market risk
in the Basel II accords (the ones whose rules about capital
requirements and suchlike the bankers were busily circum-
venting).

But there were and are problems with VAR, and the system has never been without vociferous critics. The first
problem is the same as with all probabilistic and computer-
based systems in more or less every field of human activity:
the system is only as good as its data. It's one of the most
important maxims in computing: GIGO, meaning Garbage
In, Garbage Out. There were areas in which there were
plenty of data—to do with corporate bonds and risks of
default and suchlike—and other areas where the data were
much thinner. The apparent precision of the VAR number
had an inbuilt propensity to be misleading, because it didn't
admit that it could be only as good as the data on which it
was based.

The other problem was even deeper and more consequential. The probabilities in the VAR models were based
on the bell curve. Everybody knows the bell curve, and for
a good reason, because an enormous number of phenomena fit into it, including most things about people which
can be measured—heights, weights, IQs. The bell curve,
known in mathematics as the normal distribution curve,
fits all phenomena which tend to cluster around a mean or
average. The further away from that mean, the less likely
phenomena are to occur. The normative distribution underlies all sorts of mathematics and it is central to the study of
probability.

The problem with using the bell curve here is simply
put: how do we know that the normative distribution ap-
plies to events in the financial markets? The way in which
people move and jostle around a room might be plotted

and mapped with statistical tools and shown to resemble something like a normative distribution—sometimes people are over here, sometimes they're over there, but most of the time they're somewhere in the middle. But shout "Fire!" and the movement of people in the room will look very different—it will feature a stampede toward the exits. There's nothing bell-curvy about that. How do we know that financial markets, under stress, will stick to the probability distributions plugged into the VAR models? We don't. In the words of Nassim Taleb, the first and most vociferous critic of VAR, in the course of a famous debate about the value of the models in 1997: "You're worse off relying on misleading information than on not having any information at all. If you give a pilot an altimeter that is sometimes defective he will crash the plane. Give him nothing and he will look out the window. Technology is only safe if it is flawless."[7] Taleb's disagreement with the whole idea of "engineering" risk was, and still is, profound; his disagreement with VAR especially so:

> VAR has made us replace about 2,500 years of market experience with a co-variance matrix that is still in its infancy. We made a tabula rasa of years of market lore that was picked up from trader to trader and crammed everything into a co-variance matrix. Why? So a management consultant or an unemployed electrical engineer can understand financial market risks.
>
> To me, VAR is charlatanism because it tries to estimate something that is not scientifically possible to estimate, namely the risks of rare events. It gives people misleading precision that could lead to the buildup of positions by hedgers. It lulls people to sleep.

The most lulling thing about it is the false confidence offered by the precise statements of probability: the 95 percent chance of a measurable loss, which is also the 5 percent chance of what could be total disaster. The point about VAR should have been what it couldn't tell you, the terribleness of the catastrophes which awaited just outside its confidence levels. If you have a 95 percent chance of losing less than $1,000 today and a 5 percent chance of being taken hostage, tortured, then being covered in honey and eaten alive by ants, are you likely to say, "A thousand dollars? That doesn't sound so bad!" I doubt it. But that's what many of the banks did.

The most thoughtful advocates of VAR at times sound oddly like its critics. Philippe Jorion is a California-based French economist who took part in a famous-to-quants exchange with Nassim Taleb in April 1997. Jorion made a number of measured points about the usefulness of VAR and then disagreed with Taleb about some specific issues to do with how well VAR predicted unusual and non-bell-curvy phenomena. A wobbly speedometer, Jorion said, was more useful than no speedometer at all. Then he came to this moderate and sensible-sounding conclusion:

> It seems premature to describe VAR as "charlatanism." In spite of naysayers, VAR is an essential component of sound risk management systems. VAR gives an estimate of potential losses given market risks. In the end, the greatest benefit of VAR lies in the imposition of a structured methodology for critically thinking about risk. Institutions that go through the process of computing their VAR are forced to confront their exposure to financial risks and to set up a proper risk management function. Thus the

process of getting to VAR may be as important as the number itself.

So what VAR boils down to is that it forces people to think properly about risk. We're back to where we started: to the fact that we as a species are rubbish at thinking about risk.

By the early years of the new millennium, everybody and his dog was using the new technique for assessing risk. What you thought of that depended on whether you believed critics of VAR, advocates of VAR, or managers who didn't know what they were doing. These would have told you, in order, that the financial world was sleepwalking over the edge of the Grand Canyon; that it was navigating by a rough-and-ready compass preferable to no compass at all; or that everything was fine and the bankers knew very well where they were going. Crucially, though, the idea had taken hold that the new techniques gave a way of quantifying and assessing risk and therefore of managing it. Risk could be arranged so that everything boiled down to a number.

This was why David X. Li's application of the Gaussian copula function to CDOs hit so hard.[8] Up until now the whole problem with mortgage-backed CDOs had been that they couldn't be reduced to a number. To recap, there was no national housing market in the United States; there had never been a national downturn in house prices; there were only patchy data for housing; and the new subprime mortgages were so new that there was no chance of having a historic accumulation of data, because there was no history. Li's formula came along as a magic wand to wave away all these troubles and magically solve them, thanks to its novel way of calculating correlation.

This, remember, is at the heart of the modern quanty way of investing. The power of correlation was what Harry Markowitz had taught the investing world: how you needed to understand the way prices moved, together or separately, to design a portfolio with the lowest possible level of unnecessary risk. In trying to correlate mortgage data, what was being calculated was all the diverse risks and life histories of the various U.S. subprime borrowers—a stoner dude with dodgy credit in Seattle, an immigrant family with no credit history in Arizona, a young couple with a history of maxed-out credit cards and nonpayment in Michigan. How do you make a mathematical model of that and show what's likely to happen to them and what they're likely to do under a range of different circumstances? Bearing in mind that the kind of loan they have didn't exist until about five minutes ago?

Easy—the new formula ignored the history altogether. There was one number, gamma, plugged into the formula to represent correlation, and that number was taken not from the historic analysis of mortgages but from the price of credit default swaps on those mortgages. That was Li's big idea, or one of them: instead of trying to access the underlying raw material of data on mortgage payments—which nobody could say with a straight face that they had done—quants could just ignore them and look at the way the relevant CDS prices moved. If your insurance has just got more expensive but your neighbor's has just got cheaper, your insurance and his insurance are negatively correlated. If his goes up but less than yours, there's a small positive correlation. If his goes up even more than yours, you're positively correlated, but his is more volatile. You don't (the advocates of the new formula argued) need to know all the details of exactly what's influencing the price of your two different insurance policies. Maybe you occasionally leave the door open while he's a ragingly house-proud neat freak; maybe you go away for six months and let the house to students who trash the place. Who cares? It doesn't matter, since all the relevant information is in the price. The way your insurance price moves in relation to his tells you all you need to know about how your risks and his are correlated. Since CDS is at base a form of insurance, the principle is the same. You didn't need to know the specifics of mortgage history to work out the correlations; all you needed to do was look at how the prices were correlated— and all you had to do to find the prices was look them up. Just plug those data into the Gaussian copula formula, and it will give you back a number which quantifies the level of risk you're taking.

It was magic. The Gaussian copula formula used historic CDS correlation data to create accurate—theoretically accurate—assessments of risk and thereby unlocked the whole new market of subprime CDOs. There was only one problem, and it's not just a problem apparent in hindsight, since many people warned about it at the time. The problem was that the correlation data were rubbish. Subprime mortgages were new and had never been through a severe period of market difficulty. There was simply no way of knowing what would happen if they did. Of course, there was a commonsense way of guessing what would happen, based on the permanent truth that what goes up must come down and that the housing market was obviously a bubble that was going to burst. If that happened, lots of risky new borrowers would fail to pay back their mortgages and would go into default, and since there were so many of them, there would be a precipitate crash in the housing market and an especially precipitate one in the group of people who had taken out the risky and high-yielding new loans. Since that group's mortgage payments were what was underpinning a whole new category of CDOs, that category was in for a very, very bumpy ride. That's what common sense would have suggested. But the ninja-level quantitative models used in the CDOs were precisely not based on common sense; they were based on data which were simply inadequate. Using the Gaussian copula formula and the modern edifice of risk engineering, the figure the quants came up with for the current market implosion—based on a 20 percent decline in house prices, feeding through into the CDO industry—was that it was likely to happen only in a time frame many, many trillions of years longer than the history of the universe.

You have to ask yourself how intelligent people could ever have come to persuade themselves of that. I'm only forty-seven, but this is the second time in my adult life-time—the second time in my lifetime as a mortgage-paying property owner—that property prices have fallen by more than 20 percent. It seems willful and bizarre and well over the fine line between clever and stupid for entire banks to have persuaded themselves that such a drop in U.S. home prices was not just unlikely but trillions-and-trillions-to-one unlikely. What makes this even less excusable is that equally unlikely events had happened not long before—yet the models of risk and probability had been allowed to re-main intact.

A brief word on statistics: the measure of unlikelihood in any given distribution—that's the picture made by the graph, the best known of which is our friend the bell curve—is called the standard distribution. This is a mathe-matically determined amount which tells you how much volatility, how much up-and-down and side-to-side move-ment, there is in the statistics. A school in which the stu-dents have an average IQ of 100 but a high standard deviation has some very-high-IQ kids and some very-low-IQ ones; a school with the same average IQ but a smaller standard distribution has more kids in the middle and fewer outliers. In the normal distribution, one standard deviation on either side of the average includes about 68 percent, just over two-thirds, of all the data; two standard devia-tions includes about 95 percent. Three standard deviations is 99.7 percent. Standard deviation often appears in equa-tions as the greek letter ß, sigma. It's a useful measure of how widely spread any data are, and it's also a useful mea-sure of probability. A "3-sigma event" is something that is supposed to happen only 0.3 percent of the time, i.e., about once every three thousand times something is measured.

Quants use these measures of probability all the time. According to the models in use by the quants, the Black Monday crash of 1987 was a ten-sigma event. Translated into English, that meant that, in the words of Roger Low-enstein's book *When Genius Failed: The Rise and Fall of Long-Term Capital Management*:

> Economists later figured that, on the basis of the market's historical volatility, had the market been open every day since the creation of the Universe, the odds would still have been against its falling that much in a single day. In fact, had the life of the Uni-verse been repeated one billion times, such a crash would still have been theoretically "unlikely."

The defiance of common sense here is flagrant. If your mathematical model tells you that something is impossible— which is what, in practice, that degree of improbability implies—and then that thing happens, you know with certainty that your mathematical model is wrong. It doesn't make sufficient allowance for reality. In this case, the unacknowledged reality was to do with portfolio insurance, but it doesn't in fact matter what the unacknowledged thing was; it just matters that your model doesn't work, because when unexpected things happen—and as every grown-up in the world knows, unexpected things happen all the time—the historically based mathematical model can't cope with it. If the Black Monday crash wasn't adequate to make that point, it could equally have been made by the Russian bond default of 1998 and the market panic which accompanied that. (That incident destroyed Long-Term Capital Management, the genius-only hedge fund mentioned earlier.) The 1998 default was a 7-sigma event. That means it should statistically have happened only once every 3 billion years. And it wasn't the only one. The last decades have seen numerous 5-, 6-, and 7-sigma events. Those are supposed to happen, respectively, one day in every 13,932 years, one day in every 4,039,906 years, and one day in every 3,105,395,365 years. Yet no one concluded from this that the statistical models in use were wrong.

The mathematical models simply didn't work in a crisis. They worked when they worked, which was most of the time; but the whole point of them was to assess risk, and some risks by definition happen at the edges of known likelihoods. The strange thing is that this is strongly hinted at in the VAR model, as propounded by its more philosophically minded defenders such as Philippe Jorion: it marks the boundaries of the known world, up to the VAR break, and then writes "Here be Dragons." But nobody paid enough attention to the dragons and other beasties which lay outside the boundaries of the VAR model. What they relied on

instead was historical data. The great problem with historical data is in the name: they are historical. By definition
they don't include new phenomena. They aren't like actuarial tables or charts of how tall people are, in which cases
you can reliably accumulate and measure and draw conclusions. Financial markets aren't like that: the impact of un-
certainties is just too high. In financial markets, the lesson
of history is paradoxical but clear: it is that you can't rely
on historical data.

The ultimate absurdities were reached during the early
days of the credit crunch. Remember the basic reality underlying that: people with bad credit histories, who for the
most part lied to get loans, not being able to pay back their
mortgages. Consider the case of Lashawn Wilson in Baltimore, with no job and no income, supposedly making
mortgage payments to the trustee who was the ultimate
owner of her mortgage, Citigroup Mortgage Loan Trust,
Inc., 2007-WFHE2. How likely is a problem with that and
similar mortgages? Not too unlikely, one would have
thought. But by the time the market had finished with its
packaging and securitization and CDOs and CDSs and
VAR and Gaussian copula formulae, that turned into events
which the CFO of Goldman Sachs, David Viniar, described
like this: "We were seeing things that were 25-standard-
deviation moves, several days in a row." It is almost impossible to put into words how big a number 25 sigma is,
expressed as odds to one. Twenty sigma is ten times the
number of all the particles in the known universe; 25 sigma
is the same but with the decimal point moved fifty-two
places to the right. It's equivalent to winning the U.K. national lottery twenty-one times in a row. That's the probability of a single 25-sigma event. Goldman were claiming to
experience them several days in a row. That is so wrong

you can't put it into words. It shouldn't be possible to be that wrong.[9]

Remember, what we're talking about here is a drop in house prices, which caused people with bad credit to have trouble paying their mortgages. That was turned into something that was literally the most unlikely thing to have happened in the history of the universe.

When Alan Greenspan spoke about "a flaw in the model that I perceived is the critical functioning structure that defines how the world works," that was what he was talking about. He was talking about the fact that he felt certain, as an article of faith, that markets could be relied on to accurately price and manage risk. (Pricing risk correctly is more or less the same as managing it correctly: it implies that you've got your sums right.) This was Greenspan's testimony to the House Committee on Oversight and Government Reform, the account of the crisis in the words of the most important central banker in the world, with my commentary—and my hope is that by this point in the book, you'll be able to understand him.[10]

What went wrong with global economic policies that had worked so effectively for nearly four decades?

[Well, that's one way of putting it. But it ignores the increasing inequality since the end of the Cold War and also the increasing power of the financial industry, and how it secured from willing politicians the right to deregulate itself and become more casino-like. It also ignores the near disasters such as Black Monday, the Russian debt/Long-Term Capital Management crisis, and all the other occasions which should have showed the inadequacy of mathematical

models of correlation and risk.] The breakdown has
been most apparent in the securitization of home
mortgages. The evidence strongly suggests that
without the excess demand from securitizers, subprime mortgage originations (undeniably the original
source of crisis) would have been far smaller and defaults accordingly far fewer. [All true.] But subprime
mortgages pooled and sold as securities became subject to explosive demand from investors around the
world. These mortgage backed securities being "subprime" were originally offered at what appeared to
be exceptionally high risk-adjusted market interest
rates. But with U.S. home prices still rising, delin-
quency and foreclosure rates were deceptively mod-
est. Losses were minimal. To the most sophisticated
investors in the world, they were wrongly viewed as
a "steal." The consequent surge in global demand
for U.S. subprime securities by banks, hedge, and
pension funds supported by unrealistically positive
rating designations by credit agencies was, in my
judgment, the core of the problem. [Yes.] Demand
became so aggressive that too many securitizers and
lenders believed they were able to create and sell
mortgage backed securities so quickly that they never
put their shareholders' capital at risk and hence did
not have the incentive to evaluate the credit quality
of what they were selling. [True.] Pressures on lenders to supply more "paper" collapsed subprime un-
derwriting standards from 2005 forward. Uncritical
acceptance of credit ratings by purchasers of these
toxic assets has led to huge losses. [True.]

It was the failure to properly price such risky assets that precipitated the crisis. In recent decades, a

vast risk management and pricing system has
evolved, combining the best insights of mathematicians and finance experts supported by major ad-
vances in computer and communications technology.
A Nobel Prize was awarded for the discovery of the
pricing model that underpins much of the advance in
derivates markets. This modern risk management
paradigm held sway for decades. [All true so far.]
The whole intellectual edifice, however, collapsed in
the summer of last year because the data inputted
into the risk management models generally covered
only the past two decades, a period of euphoria. Had
instead the models been fitted more appropriately to
historic periods of stress, capital requirements would
have been much higher and the financial world
would be in far better shape today, in my judgment.
[He's missing the point: it's not that the data didn't
have enough history—though they didn't—it's that
the whole idea of relying on historic data is inadequate. The unforeseen event is the unforeseen event,
by definition: if these things fitted into models, the
models would work; but they demonstrably don't
work, when faced with the unexpected. They are, in
the words of the hedge fund manager David Einhorn, "like an air bag which works all the time except when you get into a crash."]

So we can quibble with the precise details of Greenspan's hindsight view. In essence, though, he was right: the
mistake all came down to risk. He was much, much too
late, but he was right. Banking is all about the management
of risk; and in this central respect, the bankers massively
failed. They did so by relying on inaccurate mathematical

models which they themselves didn't fully understand. (Mervyn King, the governor of the Bank of England, says that CDOs "have a distribution of returns which is highly sensitive to small changes in the correlations of underlying returns which we do not understand with any great precision." [11]) The result was that they failed as utterly and completely as it is possible to fail. They weren't just wrong in practice, the way you are wrong if you call heads and a coin lands tails; they were philosophically wrong. They were exposed as doing something which was contrary to the nature of reality.

SIX

FUNNY SMELLS

The credit crunch was based on a climate, a problem, and a mistake. It was also based on a failure, that of the regulators and politicians and central bankers whose job it was to look out for the signs of economic danger. Part of this was to do with ignoring warning signs in the form of too-good-to-be true data, economic overheating, and funny smells.

Financial crashes, implosions, and scandals are always accompanied by funny smells. An example: in 2007, I went to the Cúirt International Festival of Literature in Galway city in Ireland. The previous time I'd been there was in 1999, for the annual Mass a year after my mother's death. That occasion happened to be during a solar eclipse, so the first thing that guests were given on arrival at the hotel was a set of instructions about how you were to be sure not to look at the sun. Cut to eight years later and the same hotel, and this time, no sooner had I crossed the threshold than I was given a set of instructions about how I wasn't supposed to drink the water. The water in Galway was contaminated by an outbreak of cryptosporidium, a single-celled protozoa which causes symptoms of gastroenteritis, including, says one medical dictionary, "profuse, foul smelling, watery diarrhoea, vomiting (especially in children)," and lasts for one to three weeks. There is no treatment. Nice. At the time I was mainly amused by the coincidence and also fell to wondering what would happen next time I was in town: don't look at the sky, don't drink the water, what next, don't breathe? A plague of locusts? I didn't pay nearly enough attention to the meaning of the cryptosporidium outbreak. It's grotesque that a place with a hinterland as rural as Galway and as copious a supply of fresh rainfall should have no drinkable water. The reason it didn't was that the whole area had grown so fast, and with so little planning and attention to sustainability, that the infrastructure had broken down—in this case, the water-treatment infrastructure. That should have been a glaring indicator of the crisis which was about to engulf the "Celtic Tiger," thanks to the carelessness with which its politicians had mismanaged the good years. To some of us who know and love Ireland, it was always a bad sign that the Irish economic miracle was named after an animal which doesn't exist. Only a few months on from that, and Ireland was in the worst economic contraction of any developed country since the Great Depression. Ireland, joked the *Economist* in February 2008 (or maybe that should be semijoked) is at risk of being "Rekjavik on Liffey," and it quoted a local witticism: "What's the difference between Ireland and Iceland? Six months and one letter." Just over a month later, economic figures came out showing that the annualized rate of decline in the economy was 25.5 percent. The Irish have had two of the worst things you can have in the current climate, a housing bubble and a credit bubble, all on the back of a decadelong economic boom. Now the country is in one of the worst recessions to hit a developed economy in modern times, one which is likely to get worse: if 25 percent of your gross national product and 13 percent of your employment come from house building, and house building stops, it's time to switch metaphors: Celtic Dodo? Celtic Zeppelin? Celtic Zombie? Celtic Car Crash? The undrinkable Galway water was a classic funny smell.

In fact, it's noticeable how often people who speak of or report these things refer to things smelling off or funny. The exact phrase was used to me by a man who turned down an invitation from Bernard Madoff to participate in his hedge fund. This man worked for a big investment bank, which offered clients the chance to participate in a fund-of-funds service: in other words, it offered a fund which consisted of a investments in several different hedge funds. For the banker, this should have been a win-win, because he had clients who were clamoring to join in Madoff's funds—which were famous for their consistency, returning a steady 10 to 12 percent in all years and all weather—and the inflow of money would in turn generate a steady income in fees. And Madoff was known for being choosy about his clients. (We now know the reason why: he didn't want any investors who were likely to ask the wrong sort of questions.) So there was nothing not to like . . . except that this man didn't like it. The steadiness of Madoff's returns seemed wrong. He turned down the opportunity to participate in Madoff's fund, a decision which cost him a good deal of political capital at his bank, until Madoff was exposed as a fraudster (and the banker who turned him down was promoted). Why did he turn down Madoff? "Because it just didn't smell right."

Funny smells come in a variety of types. The funny smells surrounding the credit crunch were not for the most

part to do with fraud—though having said that, a CDO investor who had had a long look at the way mortgages were
being originated would have been gagging on fraud-related
stench. Mainly, they were funny smells to do with things
which were just too good to be true. That is a critically important category of funny smells, and it is the kind which is
most relevant in the story of the credit crunch. It is a category of funny smell which involves an element of the willful, or of wishful thinking; or perhaps just of ignoring
what's in front of your nose. To adopt a metaphor I heard
used by the chancellor of the Exchequer, Alistair Darling,
it's a bit like putting flowers in the hallway as a solution to
the problem of dry rot.

There are people whose job it is to sniff out funny
smells, to think about them and what they mean, and to
make plans about them on our behalf. They are the central
bankers. There is a passage in Norman Mailer's novel *Har-
lot's Ghost* in which the narrator rhapsodizes about the
CIA being "the mind of America." Central bankers are a
little like that. Their job is to notice everything and think
about everything—everything economic—and then to act
on it via one tool and one tool only: the interest rate.* This
determines, or anyway influences, the level of borrowing,
the level of credit, the level of economic activity, the level of
inflation, the level of unemployment, the speed of growth,

---

* This is an oversimplification, because, as the current crisis has shown,
central banks can also print money and do so via a number of mecha-
nisms such as the new favorite, "quantitative easing." This is essentially
buying its own debt instruments without issuing anything to back it up;
it's not literally the same thing as printing money but it's as good as. It is a
measure that's resorted to when interest rates have been cut so much or so
fast that there's nowhere else to go with them. All this is a response to a
desperate crisis and is a sign that all normal measures have failed. Under
normal circumstances, the interest rate is the whole ball game.

the exchange rate, the whole kaboodle, but it is also a fairly crude tool: it's as if the central banker were sitting at a desk console with thousands of flashing lights and digital read-outs and heads-up visual displays, all pouring in overwhelming quantities of data, and in response to it the banker can move only one lever, in a straight line backward or forward, and preferably only a very little at a time.

That's the job of central banking. I've already said that the most influential central banker in the world, in the lead-up to the credit crunch, was Alan Greenspan, and I've mentioned the dogmatic laissez-faire ideology (underpinned by Ayn Rand's Objectivism) for which he is famous. I haven't mentioned that one of his traits was an extraordinary nose for and attention to detail. During his tenure at the Fed, Greenspan was legendary for his ability to vacuum up gigantic amounts of raw data and bring them to bear in his assessment of the desired movements in interest rates. The account I've given of him so far might make him sound like a man committed to abstractions, but it must be stressed that Greenspan's attention to practical detail and to what the facts were telling him was at the heart of what he did. Funny smells were what he was all about.

As for the specific risks of a bubble in house prices, Greenspan was well aware of the dangers. Or at least there had been a time when that was true. Talking to American real estate agents in 1995, he said that "It is hard to overestimate the importance of house price trends for consumer psyches and behavior. . . . Consumers view their home equity as a cushion or security blanket against the possibility of future hard times."[1] That seems unequivocal: the importance of house prices is "hard to overestimate." But this raises the question of why he went on to ignore them so hard for so long. It was the bubble in house prices which both caused people to pile into the housing market and then to lose their shirts when it popped. That bubble was based on low interest rates, and the man responsible for setting those low rates was Greenspan. I've mentioned the chronology already: the years of the "Goldilocks economy" and "Great Moderation," growing neither too hot nor too cold, during which interest rates never moved by more than 0.25 percent at any time.

During these years the markets came up with the phrase "the Greenspan put" to describe the Fed chairman's apparent determination to protect share prices. A "put" is an option to sell shares, so "the Greenspan put" implied that Greenspan would always be there to bail out the market if it fell—which was a little paradoxical, because he had famously warned, as early as 1996, about "irrational exuberance" in the stock market. But he seemed to say one thing and do another, because if he wanted to chill that exuberance, a couple of sharp jolts to the interest rate, combined with a scary speech or two, would have done the trick. It's almost impossible to exaggerate the prestige and influence Greenspan had in the markets during those years. In the words of Judge Richard Posner's book *A Failure of Capitalism:* "Greenspan's tremendous prestige gave him a largely free hand, which he did not use, to choke off the housing bubble by raising interest rates and to rein in risky lending by exercising more assertively the control that the Federal Reserve has over commercial banks. He thought he could avoid political controversy by waiting for bubbles to form and pop and clearing up afterwards by lowering interest rates." There was an element of mutual admiration to all this: Greenspan loved the doctrinally pure free markets, and the doctrinally pure free markets loved him. That, in turn, was the reason why he was and would continue to be reluctant to burst any bubbles: who was he to interfere in the operation of the market, which by definition was wiser about itself than any individual could be? The free market was She Who Must Be Obeyed, and if the market wanted to have a bubble, a bubble it must have.

Then came the dot-com crash, followed by the implosion of Enron. And that is the point at which hindsight sees Greenspan as having gone off the rails. On January 3, 2001, he broke with his policy of slow-and-steady movements in the interest rates and cut them by half a percent in one go, down to 6 percent, and followed in the subsequent months with further rate cuts—this being an example of the Greenspan put in its most flagrant form. After all, if the markets were irrationally exuberant in 1996 and had kept going up, why wouldn't a crash, even one leading to a small recession, be desirable? The best analogy is to the management of forestry in a dry, hot country. The landscape needs fires—preferably small ones at regular and not-too-frequent intervals. If it doesn't get them, the undergrowth builds up and offers a dangerously copious supply of fuel for the big fire when it eventually and inevitably comes. Had Greenspan fallen a little in love with his own publicity, as the all-knowing seer whose superbly judged nudges on the levers of interest rates had never been equaled? Or perhaps he had come to believe the hype about the new financial instruments, as he seemed to be saying in a speech a year after his comments on "irrational exuberance," when he said that we were witnessing the dawn of "a new paradigm of active credit management." In either case, he seemed to have forgotten the old principle, much quoted by my father, that "all you need to be an investment genius is a short memory and a rising market." We won't know what Greenspan was really thinking and he certainly wouldn't say; whatever it was, commentators were beginning to wonder whether interest rates had been cut too far, too fast. By 2003, the rate was 1 percent, and it stayed there for a year, even after the economy started growing at an annualized rate of 7.5 percent.[2] Is it any wonder a bubble built up? For the reasons already given, it wasn't a bubble in stocks or bonds but in assets.

The "asset price bubble" is economist-speak for the housing bubble. During the years of the buildup, while interest rates were low and debt was cheap, people borrowed cheap money and poured it into houses; or they took money out of their houses by taking out loans against the increased value of those houses, treating them as if they were giant ATM machines. They then spent it on whatever they spent it on, as described by Greenspan in 1995. The point to bear in mind here is that the credit bubble, the debt bubble, the asset price bubble, and the housing bubble were all basically the same phenomenon.

In Greenspan's account of the causes of the crisis quoted at the end of the last chapter, he doesn't mention low interest rates and the housing price bubble; they are conspicuously absent as contributing factors from all the self-justification he's given since the crisis. When he does blame someone for the bubble, he tends to blame China. His argument is that interest rates stayed low not because he (and other central bankers) kept them low but because the Chinese were buying up so many T-bills that there was no reason for the prices to rise. History will, I believe, judge this view to be mainly incorrect and say that the blame for the asset price bubble was about 90 percent to do with central bankers ignoring the dangers of low interest rates for too long. This was the first of the crucial funny smells ignored by Greenspan. He was far from alone, though. Chi-

nese saving can't take either the credit or the blame for the
interest rate/asset bubble phenomena which took place in
the United Kingdom or the European Union: China's savings were overwhelmingly in the United States. Niall Ferguson has called the resulting economic hybrid "Chimerica." [3]
I don't think there's any historical parallel for this new
transnational economic entity, and the look of it, frankly,
gives me the willies: there's something profoundly unnatu-
ral about such a skewed trans-Pacific balance of saving and
spending. The Chinese would, I suspect, dearly love to
dump a significant proportion of the T-bills and diversify
into other areas of savings, but they can't, because it would
be an act of economic mutually assured destruction: the
dollar would crash, which would wipe out (a) American
consumption and (b) Chinese savings, with consequences
roughly equal to a smallish world war.

But the European Union had no equivalent phenomenon and therefore no China to blame; and, as Greenspan
points out in that piece, it also had historically low interest rates. It had a doozy of a bubble, too, though it was
one which was concentrated on specific countries such as
Spain and Ireland. Lovely though it would be to blame the
Chinese, we can't. As for the United Kingdom, our interest
rates were higher than either the United States' or the European Union's during the relevant years. We nonetheless
had an absolute corker of a housing bubble. What could
the government or the Bank of England have done about
that? Well, the government could have pursued a set of policies designed to cool things off: allowing councils to build
more homes; loosening the planning system to make it easier to build new accommodation; abolishing mortgage relief on buy-to-let properties, and thus putting the brakes on
one of the main areas of speculative activity; uttering dark

threats about the introduction of property-based taxes. But the housing bubble translated so directly into consumer spending, and the consumer spending translated so directly into a growing economy, and the growing economy (even if it was growing unsustainably) translated so directly into a paradise of raised government spending and relatively unraised taxes, that the government—which in this case means Gordon Brown, chancellor and de facto head of domestic policy during the boom—found it unincumbent on him to act. It is easy to be critical and correct to be critical; though it should also be admitted that very few chancellors in his position at the moment would have refused such a lavish free lunch. About the only person who could possibly have exerted any serious pressure on Brown to do otherwise was the governor of the Bank of England, "Steady Eddie" George up to 2003, and Mervyn King since then.

The trouble was that King's remit to act was crucially, and in retrospect fatally, flawed. In 1997, immediately on coming into office, the new Labour government had given the Bank of England complete independence over the management of inflation and the setting of interest rates. Inflation was to be 2 percent, with a permitted margin of error of 1 percent in either direction, and if it wasn't, well, then the head of the Bank would have to . . . would have to . . . would have to *jolly well write a lette*r to the chancellor to explain why it wasn't. (I love the idea of having to write a letter when you'd prefer not to as the ultimate sanction.) The body which sets the interest rates is called the Monetary Policy Committee, and the process of voting on the interest rates is transparent, with the voting made public a few weeks after it takes place, so the markets can see the committee's balance of thinking—thus helping to avoid nasty surprises with subsequent rate changes. It's an interesting sidelight on how government in Britain works: when something really does have important consequences—such as interest rates—it's too important to faff about with the usual layers of needless secrecy. The new economic structure was announced on Tuesday, May 6, 1997, despite not having been mentioned, or even implied or hinted at, in the Labour Party's manifesto for the general election, which took place on Thursday, May 1; the most important economic initiative ever to have been imposed on the British public without any democratic consultation.

The power to set interest rates had been something of a Holy Grail for those economists who argued that the management of inflation was too important a matter to be left to politicians. I've been writing about interest rates and inflation in the way that economists usually do, as if they were matters of technical management of the economy, but another way of thinking of them is in terms of whom they directly benefit and whom they directly punish. For people on fixed incomes, inflation is a disaster, whereas for government employees and others with incomes protected against inflation it is much more neutral; for middle-class savers, it can be catastrophic; for people in debt, it can bring either ruin or—if their debt is of a fixed amount, one whose real value will go down as inflation eats it up—it can be a godsend. In a country with a minimum wage, inflation doesn't hurt the poor nearly as badly as in a country without; in fact, it can even help them, if they have debts, by making those debts worth less in real terms. Similarly, the indebted middle-class home owner can benefit from inflation, because it makes the value of her mortgage smaller; on the other hand, if the same middle-class home owner is in the unfortunate position of having lent other people money, she has a problem, because when that amount is paid back it will be worth less than it was when it was lent.

These aren't abstract issues. Individual lives become easier or harder as interest rates and inflation do their dance: they take away from some and give to others. The classic example—every economist's favorite horror story—is that of Germany and the hyperinflation that overtook it after the First World War. By the early 1920s, the German economy, damaged by defeat, had become crippled by the attempt to pay the reparations demanded by the victorious European allies and simultaneously develop a social welfare state. The government printed as much money as it could, and inflation was running out of control. In 1914, the German mark had stood at 4.2 to the dollar; by 1922, it was 190 to the dollar; by the end of that year, it was 7,600. By November 1923, a dollar was worth 630 billion marks, a loaf of bread cost 140 billion marks, and Germany was disintegrating under the strain—which was a significant contributor, perhaps even the main contributor, to the rise of the Nazis.

The giving up of control over interest rates was therefore an epochal moment for both the U.K. government and the Bank of England. But in return for becoming so powerful in that respect, the Bank had to give something back, and that was its direct supervisory role over banks and financial institutions. That was now the responsibility of the Financial Services Authority, the FSA. This was a body born after the collapse of Barings Bank, when it was felt self-evident that the banking industry's attempts at self-regulation weren't working and some external supervision was needed. As so often happens in public life, the body set up to supervise the business consisted largely of insiders (in this case, from the financial services industry) and civil ser-

vants, with representatives of the public absent. The institution carried the watermark of its origins, as institutions
tend to do: it wasn't proactive in its view of the industry
and didn't see itself as looking at the operation of the business from the outside. Regulatory bodies should have access to the perspective of outsiders looking in at the industry
from its periphery and prepared to ask obvious, which
sometimes means obviously unpopular, questions. The FSA
wasn't like that: it didn't have somebody saying "I don't
understand, please explain." It was dedicated to what
was often called the principle of "light touch" regulation.
As Adair Turner, the head of the FSA, said in his postcrash
report:

> An underlying assumption of financial regulation
> in the US, the UK and across the world, has been
> that financial innovation is by definition beneficial,
> since market discipline will winnow out any unnec-
> essary or value destructive innovations. As a result,
> regulators have not considered it their role to judge
> the value of different financial products, and they
> have in general avoided direct product regulation,
> certainly in wholesale markets with sophisticated in-
> vestors.[4]

This didn't mean that nobody at the FSA, the Bank, or
the Treasury—the third pillar of the "tripartite" regulatory
system supposed to run the British financial system—had a
clue what was happening. Many individuals thought that
debt and leverage were running at dangerously high levels.
But the trouble was that nobody felt a need to own the
problem. The Bank's responsibility for this kind of thing
had been taken away from it; the FSA was basically an in-

dustry body, which thought that the industry and market discipline would keep itself on track, with the occasional quiet word and gentle nudge on the tiller; the Treasury was in the hands of political masters who were the principal beneficiaries of the boom and who had no incentive to go around raining on parades, bursting bubbles, and telling the permanent and permanently unwelcome truth that what goes up must come down. It wasn't that everybody was asleep at the wheel; it was that no one wanted the responsibility of grabbing the wheel and changing course.

Regulation, and the lack of it and slack enforcement of it, was central to the crunch. In fact, many students of the crunch think this is the central issue in the crisis. Accounts of the banking-and-credit crisis tend to focus their explanations, which usually also means their blame, on one or more of the following four factors: greed, stupidity, government, or the banks. The process resembles a children's game in which you spin an arrow and it lands on a word. You can spin more than once. Many people who play the game land on government. When they do that, the issue they're focusing on is that of regulation. Their argument, put forcefully by Judge Richard A. Posner, is that "We are learning from [the crisis] that we need a more active and intelligent government to keep our model of a capitalist economy from running off the rails. The movement to de-regulate the financial industry went too far by exaggerating the resilience—the self-healing powers—of laissez-faire capitalism." [5]

The financial industry caused the crisis, but it could not have happened without the help of the governments, which spent decades committed to the idea of pure laissez-faire capitalism. What that ideology did, in practice, was essentially to allow bankers to write their own rules—or their lack of rules. There was a decades-long process of de-regulation and opening up, of stripping out all measures designed to second-guess the financial world's ability to regulate itself via "market discipline." This played out in a number of ways. One of these took the form of unregulation. That's what happens when a new product comes along and the industry lobbies for the new product to be set loose in the markets without much (or ideally any) regulatory supervision. One of the critical examples of this has to do with the new derivatives. CDSs and CDOs were not inscribed on stone tablets and handed down from on high, they were invented, and their function in the marketplace was something for which the banks which created them fought hard, in the face of initial skepticism from regulators and occasional anxious noises from politicians. The first set of Basel accords had been drafted before derivatives expanded to their new importance. The banks saw in that fact both the threat that governments might step in to legislate the huge new market and an opportunity to step in first and write their own rule book. The result was the creation in 1985 of the International Swaps and Derivatives Association, a trade body set up by the big international banks. Over subsequent years the ISDA fought and won a series of battles with various regulators and won the right to regulate itself.

It helped that derivatives had a swooningly ardent admirer in the head of the Federal Reserve. Step forward Alan Greenspan. "By far the most significant invention in finance during the past decade has been the extraordinary development and expansion of financial derivatives," Greenspan said in a 1999 speech given in the very Boca Raton hotel where the J.P. Morgan team had got plastered and invented the CDS. "The fact that the OTC [over-the-counter] markets function quite effectively without the benefits of [regulation] provides a strong argument for development of a less burdensome regime for exchange-traded financial derivatives. . . . These new financial instruments . . . enhance the ability to differentiate risk and allocate it to those investors most able and willing to take it."[6] Admittedly, this is the sort of thing that a computer program written to impersonate Alan Greenspan would have said: Free market good. Trust free market. More free market. As so often with the ideologically committed free marketeer, there is no sense that he's actually thinking about what he's saying: he's merely adumbrating arguments toward a conclusion he had reached in advance.

A big advantage held by the banks here was that legislators had next to no idea what derivatives were or how they worked; there was something lulling and seductive about the idea that the banks should be allowed to police themselves, thanks to self-regulation and, of course, "market discipline." So the banks' lobbying had an attentive, even grateful, audience. The campaign was so effective that it didn't just succeed in persuading legislators not to legislate; the derivatives lobby went one better than that. It managed to get Congress to pass a law actually *banning* legislation. In 2000, it passed the Commodity Futures Modernization Act, which among other things asserted that CDSs were not futures or options and were therefore exempt from regulation; it also added provisos protecting the trade of derivatives over the counter, that is, from one party to another rather than through an exchange. The great disadvantage of over-the-counter trades is that they are unmonitored, and no one knows what the risks are and where they are being spread—but they were much quicker and more convenient for the banks, and that was all that mattered. This is one of the critically important areas which is going to require reregulation, since the financial system badly needs the degree of control and supervision which could be created by trading CDSs through a regulated exchange. Note that the 2000 bill—which also included a clause exempting Enron's energy derivatives business from legislation, the "Enron loophole," as it's known—passed through both the Senate and the House of Representatives without debate.

This, and the issue of derivatives more generally, is one of the points where the funny smells could have built up to such an extent that they created a counterfactual. Maybe this was a road not taken, an alternative path which did not lead to the present we've just been living through. Why should derivatives be traded over the counter at all? Even a layperson can immediately see the risks in having contracts of such immense value knocking around the system, unregulated and indeed not even counted by any central authority. How on earth did we get to such a place of total free-for-all? We could start with the 1982 Garn–St. Germain Depository Institutions Act, a bill signed into law by Ronald Reagan with the pronouncement that it was "the most important legislation for financial institutions in the last fifty years. It provides a long-term solution for troubled thrift institutions." President Reagan concluded, "All in all, I think we hit the jackpot." In fact, what happened was that the bill, by creating insurance for mortgage lenders, increased their recklessness and led directly to the savings and loan crash of the early 1980s, with a cost to the taxpayer of $124.6 billion. It was this bill which stood at the beginning of two and a half decades of consistent deregulation and loosening of regulatory supervision—and all the subsequent legislation moved in the same direction.

The general tide of deregulation and unregulation was brilliantly summed up in the aforementioned article, "The Quiet Coup," by Simon Johnson, a professor at MIT who was formerly the head economist of the International Monetary Fund. In that role, his day job involved going into crisis-struck countries and banging politicians' heads together to get them to accept reforms as a price of IMF aid. He acquired an extensive experience of countries which had been effectively captured by a ruling elite which governed entirely in its own interests. His startling conclusion about the current crisis is that the United States has become one of those countries. As the banking sector got richer, its power and influence over U.S. government policy increased—power and influence which the bankers weren't at all too afraid to use. So the current crisis was caused by the banking sector's excessive influence on U.S. government policy; what he calls in the title of the piece "the quiet coup." This is his summary of what the bankers asked for and got:

From this confluence of campaign finance, personal connections, and ideology there flowed, in just the past decade, a river of deregulatory policies that is, in hindsight, astonishing:

- insistence on free movement of capital across borders
- the repeal of Depression-era regulations separating commercial and investment banking
- a congressional ban on the regulation of credit-default swaps
- major increases in the amount of leverage allowed to investment banks
- a light (dare I say invisible?) hand at the Securities and Exchange Commission in its regulatory enforcement

- an international agreement to allow banks to measure their own riskiness
- and an intentional failure to update regulations so as to keep up with the tremendous pace of financial innovation[7]

The undoing of the Depression-era banking legislation was a critical component in this. In the aftermath of the Great Depression, the populist anger at banks and the financial system led to a series of laws designed to ensure that nothing like the crash would ever happen again. That is a generally applicable historic pattern: societies tend to regulate their financial systems only in the aftermath of a scary failure. Conversely, when markets are booming, legislation tends to loosen, and so does enforcement of the existing legislation. The centerpiece of the Depression-era legislation was the Glass-Steagall Act of 1933, which separated investment banking (the casino, where the bank makes bets on its own behalf) and commercial banking (the piggy bank, where ordinary Joes deposit their savings and the bank lends it to other ordinary Joes to buy houses and cars and invest in their businesses). The idea was to let investment banks do their thing and blow themselves up without impacting on the general public. This hampered the freedom of the banks, not as a by-product of the act but as part of its central intention, and not surprisingly, it was never loved by bankers. When the long boom began in 1982, the Act came under pressure from lobbyists, who exerted particular pressure over the point that it was unfair to banks, because they were now competing with a plethora of other nonbank financial institutions which weren't subject to the same rules.

They were making a valid point, but they were making

it the wrong way around. It was certainly true that the banks were now operating in a crowded financial marketplace in which many of the most important institutions weren't old-school banks. The bankers looked at this fact and drew the conclusion that what was needed was less legislation, so that the banks—the banks proper—would be competing on a level playing field with all the other financial intermediaries. In retrospect this was precisely wrong; what was needed was for a much more active and intrusive legislative regime to check risk and leverage within all financial intermediaries (which from now on I'm going to go back to calling "banks"). But the bankers and their pet legislators drew the opposite conclusion. So Glass-Steagall was abolished in 1999, thanks to a bill sponsored by three Republicans and backed by Treasury Secretary Larry Summers. Only eight senators voted against the bill, one of them Byron Dorgan, who said, "This bill will in my judgment raise the likelihood of future massive taxpayer bailouts." Looking back on the amazing correctness of this prediction from a decade later, Dorgan observed, "The culture is that Wall Street knows best." The proliferation of nonbank banks grew and grew. As Timothy Geithner, President Obama's Treasury secretary, pointed out, by 2007 more than half of America's banking was being handled by a "parallel financial system" of largely unregulated institutions. These institutions were, in Geithner's words, "vulnerable to a classic type of run, but without the protections such as deposit insurance that the banking system has in place to reduce such risks." [8]

The culture which led to this point was not the exclusive property of one party or one section of the political elite; it was simply the received wisdom of the people in charge. It's for this reason that although Alan Greenspan can be blamed for specific mistakes, he can't take the rap for the financial crisis overall. The entire climate of opinion, in the world of power, was in favor of laissez-faire, deregulation, and "innovation," so if it hadn't been Greenspan advocating this ideology, pushing through the policies which enacted it, and in turn earning the love and trust of the markets and loving and trusting them back, it would have been someone else. That was the system.

A big part of the problem was also that existing laws which might have been brought to bear weren't. There are two aspects of financial regulation, the laws themselves and how they are used: call them the framework and the regime. In the United States, the framework was undermined by decades of deregulation, and had become a dementedly fragmented and patchworky thing. U.S. banks, for instance, are regulated by the Office of Thrift Supervision, the state banking regulators, the Office of the Comptroller of the Currency, the Federal Reserve, the Federal Deposit Insurance Corporation, the National Credit Union Administration, and (if the bank is participating in TARP) by the Treasury; and bearing in mind the broad definition of banks to include other financial intermediaries, they are also likely to have dealings with the other regulatory bodies that have a say in the running of financial institutions, such as the state insurance regulators, the Commodity Futures Trading Commission, the Financial Industry Regulatory Authority, the state securities regulators (every state has one), the state attorney generals (who sometimes take an interest that the markets would prefer they didn't), and the big daddy of the stock markets, the Securities and Exchange Commission, or SEC.[9] They are also regulated by the various agencies in the various overseas markets in which they operate. This is a major case of alphabet soup, and it reminds me of something I once heard a political scientist say about Italy. That country, he said, makes you understand what an anarchy would in practice look like: it wouldn't be a society with no laws but one with thousands of laws to which nobody pays any attention.

It is a moot point whether a system as complicated and fragmentary as that can be, to use the jargon, "fit for purpose." (President Obama's plans to clean up financial regulation, announced on June 16, 2009, give the Treasury more powers but don't clean up the regulatory tangle. That decision reflects political realities about turf but might not be the best one in the long term.) Even if it were the best framework in the world, however, there would be a question of the regime which was administering it—and that has, in recent decades, been a problem. Things always get too lax in boom years. That's a fact of psychology. Add to it an ideological belief that the markets know best and that government's duty is to shrink itself as small as possible, and you have a recipe for regulators not exactly to look the other way but to take a shrugging, boys-will-be-boys attitude to actions which look irregular.

Sometimes this involves making new rules to suit the banks. In a meeting on April 2004,[10] the SEC agreed to allow the five big banks to cut the amount of capital they had to hold in reserve against potential losses in its investments. The banks involved were Merrill Lynch, Goldman Sachs, Lehman Brothers, JPMorgan Chase, and Bear Stearns. Three of those banks no longer exist, and the other two had to end (temporarily, it turned out) their status as investment banks; *none of that would have happened* if the SEC had not changed the rules that day. The change allowed the banks to increase their leverage hugely—Bear Stearns, for instance, increased its leverage to the point where it had $33 in debt for every $1 in equity.

There was supposed to be a quid pro quo for the change. It was brought in because the European Commission was threatening to regulate the U.S. banks that had brokerage operations in Europe—in other words, to extend its legislative remit from the subsidiary stockbroking companies up to the banks that owned them. But the Commission agreed not to do that if the SEC took the parent companies—not just the brokerages, which it already supervised—under its legislative remit. The SEC agreed and the banks agreed too, the deal being that they were allowed to relax the rules on how much capital they kept in reserve. In return the SEC was allowed access to their books to monitor and assess their risks. By this point, the reader will have no trouble in guessing what happened. The banks took their relaxed capital rules, and the SEC in return did nothing. Its investigations were tentative, and when the seven-strong team of investigators did find potential problems—mainly to do with risk, as of course they would be—the concerns were ignored by senior managers. As of October 2008, four and a half years after the April 2004 meeting, the SEC had not completed a single investigation in the last eighteen months.[11] In other words, the banks got the rule change they needed to take gigantic risks, and in return, the SEC got the power it needed to supervise them and didn't use it.

That was the regime at the body which was supposed to be regulating the banks. Just as President Bush's Environmental Protection Agency and Consumer Product Safety Commission seemed to have been captured by the very interests they were supposed to be regulating, so it was at the SEC. Much of this doctrinaire laissez-faire involved the nonenforcement of the rules which already existed. An activist SEC, for instance, would never have allowed Bernard Madoff to run his Ponzi scheme; the very consistency of his returns—the funny smell alluded to above—would have been enough to draw their close attention to his accounts. In 2005, a professional investor named Harry Markopolos, a mild-mannered Boston accountant, wrote a twenty-one-page letter to the SEC, pointing out the high probability that Madoff's fund was a Ponzi scheme. The only alternative explanation Markopolos could come up with wasn't that Madoff was legit; it was that he was doing something called "front running," using private information gleaned from his stockbroking operation to make profits for his other funds. Markopolos had been in touch with the SEC about Madoff off and on since 1999, with precisely no effect.[12] Markopolos lived in some fear during the intervening years; he was scared of Madoff and of what might happen if he found out that Markopolos was onto him. As for the SEC, his judgment went beyond scathing: "My experiences with other SEC officials proved to be a systemic disappointment and led me to conclude that the SEC securities lawyers, if only through their investigative ineptitude and financial illiteracy, colluded to maintain large frauds such as the one to which Madoff later confessed."[13] That's an extraordinary charge: that the SEC was so lousy at its job that it in effect colluded with fraud. Add that to a regulatory framework full of holes and a government with an ideological commitment to letting boys be boys in the free market, and you have a perfect formula for not just ignoring funny smells but denying that they are possible.

When we look at who could have done something about this, there are two sets of people who might have raised the alarm: economists and journalists. It's more or less against the law ever to praise the media for anything, but the fact is that print journalists did speak up in public about the risks building up and the vulnerability of the global financial system. Larry Elliott in *The Guardian,* Martin Wolf and Gillian Tett in the *Financial Times,* and even the often overly gung ho *Economist* all warned about the dangers— and had the satisfaction denied to Cassandra of everyone realizing that they'd been right all along. (Remember, Cassandra's curse was that no one would believe her.) It may be, as Judge Richard Posner has observed, that journalists have a built-in affinity for narratives of disaster and collapse: the press, as he puts it, "thrives on drama and therefore conflict and alarms, discord and discontinuities." [14] (It's also true, of course, that there were industrial quantities of property market puffery and hype, a considerable amount of which took place on television.) I can't claim to have been onto this story early, but once I started working on it in the late summer of 2007, it was immediately clear to me that the global banking system was facing a structural crisis. If it was clear to me, why wasn't it as obvious to the people in charge of the economy and to the people whose job it is to advise them? It's the kind of question Daniel Kahneman has profitably studied. There is some really interesting work being done in the field of psychology and engineering (where it deeply matters) about "expert overconfidence": the likelihood of experts in a field to place too high a confidence in their own judgments. It may be that the reason why some journalists were more alert to the imminent crunch than their betters were was because of expert overconfidence combined with an overreliance on the idea that because a crisis of this sort hadn't happened, it therefore couldn't happen.

This may be why economists did as poorly as they did in forecasting the crunch. There is a sour joke among financial types, referring to the chronic pessimism and downspeak of economics, "the dismal science": they say that "economists have predicted seven of the last three down-turns." Ho ho. But they sure didn't predict this one. Just to repeat the basic point: a 20 percent drop in U.S. home prices, not on the face of it an extraordinarily unlikely thing, was enough to cause a global banking crisis that nearly destroyed the entire system, followed by a global recession verging on depression. So why didn't more economists seem aware of that possibility? Has the profession really drifted that far away from the real world? The short answer is that with some stellar exceptions—Robert Shiller, Nouriel Roubini, Paul Krugman, and John Kay conspicuous among them—yes, it has. The profession's preference for textbook-perfect academic models of phenomena led to it being AWOL during the biggest economic crisis since the 1930s. A profession whose job it is to make sense of economic phenomena collectively failed. In the words of an American university provost, "I have an entire department of economists who can provide a brilliant ex post facto explanation of what happened—and not a single one of them saw it coming in advance." Economists no longer have much interest in funny smells. The crisis exposed the profession as being a little like the British army at Singapore, its guns pointed in the wrong direction.

This failure in turn contributed to the crisis being worse than it needed to be in Britain. The Bank of England and the FSA were sluggish when they needed to be decisive, both in the early days at the time of the collapse of Northern Rock, then in the months between that and the next phase of the banking crisis in 2008. Where were the requirements to increase capital reserves, to disclose risky assets, to prepare for the storm which was obviously coming? Even if they didn't think a storm was coming, why was there so little preparation for the possibility that it might?

In the United States, the Bush administration's general laissez-faire torpor and the alphabet soup of regulatory agencies provides part of the explanation. But in the United Kingdom we don't have either of those excuses, and indeed, by comparison, our regulatory division of labor is a model of clarity: the Bank of England is supposed to look after systemic risk, while the FSA attends to the position of specific companies. But a risk which arose in specific companies and spread to the system somehow managed to squeeze through the cracks of a framework which wasn't supposed to have any cracks.

So although things should have been better in the United Kingdom, they have turned out to be as bad or worse. The one thing we haven't had is a glaring fraud of the Madoff type—not yet, anyway. But the striking thing about Simon Johnson's financial industry wish list, cited above, is that once you change the name of the Securities and Exchange Commission to the Financial Services Authority, you can apply all the rest of it word for word. The consequences for our economy are even bigger than in the United States, because financial services are a proportionately larger part of our economy. Nobody planned for that to happen; I heard that from the lips of the chancellor of the Exchequer himself. But the fact is that after Margaret Thatcher came to power, the financial sector underwent a three-decade-long expansion, during which it got everything it asked for from the government. The abolition of exchange controls in 1979 and the increasingly international flow of capital, combining with the abolition of restrictions on trading practices which culminated in the "Big Bang" in 1986, have all led to the City's increasing dominance of British economic life. The Big Bang in turn caused the "Wimbledonization" of the City, making it a place where most of the major players were foreign. As for the Big Bang, it consisted of a series of rule changes which boiled down to one simple thing: the biggest act of deregulation the financial sector had ever seen.

Because financial deregulation has been a primary culprit in the current crisis, there's a temptation to act as if it is inherently a bad thing. You need a short memory to think that. I grew up abroad and can vividly remember what a pain in the backside things such as currency restrictions were. When Margaret Thatcher came to power, you couldn't take more than £500 out of the country at any one time—a restriction which now seems as distant as that of whalebone corsetry. The City of London was a club, and a particularly unlovable club at that, exclusively white and male and not just conservative but actively reactionary as a social force. Big Bang changed both the clublike nature of City life and also its impact on Britain: global finance was now a radical force, remaking Britain in the image of a laissez-faire free-market economy, tearing up the consensual, all-in-it-together model of governance which both parties had been pursuing since the Second World War. To many observers Margaret Thatcher seemed as pure a nineteenth-century Manchester School liberal as had ever held office: keen on free trade, keen on the distinction between the deserving and the undeserving poor, and keen to make money take the place of class as the determining principle of British life.

The themes embodied by Margaret Thatcher—free trade, deregulation, and the power of finance—were not new ones in British history. What was new was the extent to which financial interests were not just important but uncontestedly paramount. A lot of British economic history concerns the struggle between the financial and industrial

interests—between the City and men from the Midlands—
and a good deal of that history boils down to a sense of
grievance and misunderstoodness on the part of Britain's
manufacturers. From the point of view of people who make
things, the City always wants to make its money too
quickly and too irresponsibly; it wants to take too big a
share of the business in return for its capital, is impatient
with slow growth, doesn't understand the importance of investment and of relationships, and wants only to achieve a
spectacular casino-like payout in the shortest possible
amount of time. The reciprocal view, from the City, has
been that manufacturers whine all the time, that they lost
the ability to control their workforces and allowed themselves to be held hostage by unions, that they had a farmer-
like tendency to complain about trading conditions in all
weathers ("The pound's too high! No one can afford our
stuff!"; "The pound's too low! We can't afford raw materi-
als!"), and that they were obtuse about the fact that the
final point of all business is to make money and that everything else is a means to that end.

That was the most important cultural difference. There
is a profound anthropological and cultural difference between an industry and a business. An industry is an entity
which as its primary purpose makes or does something and
makes money as a by-product. The car industry makes cars,
the television industry makes TV programs, the publishing
industry makes books, and with a bit of luck they all make
money too, but for the most part the people engaged in
them don't regard money as the ultimate purpose and justi-
fication of what they do. Money is a by-product of the business, rather than its fundamental raison d'être. Who goes
to work in the morning thinking that the most important
thing he's going to do that day is to maximize shareholder

value? Ideologists of capital sometimes seem to think that that's what we should be doing—which only goes to show how out of touch they are. Most human enterprises, especially the most worthwhile and meaningful ones, are in that sense industries, focused primarily on doing what they do; health care and education are both, from this anthropological perspective, industries.

At least that's what they are from the point of view of the people who work in them. But many of these enterprises are increasingly owned by people who view them not as industries but as businesses: and the purpose of a business is, purely and simply, to make money. The attitudes of a business owner are different from those of people who work in an industry, and from the point of view of business, an industry's ways of doing things are often the unexamined inheritance of the past, willfully inefficient, willfully indifferent to fundamental realities of how the world works. Money doesn't care what industry it is involved in, it just wants to make more money, and the specifics of how it does are, if not exactly a source of unconcern, very much a means to an end: the return on capital is the most important fact, and the human or cultural details involved are just that, no more than details. To workers in an industry, the attitudes and thinking of business are often summed up by the shorthand term "accountants," as in, we want to do such-and-such but the accountants won't let us, or such-and-such used to work well but then the accountants got hold of it. Hollywood, for instance, used to be an industry, involved primarily in making films, in the days when it made many more of them; now it is a business, whose primary preoccupation is to make money. The films are bigger and stupider and there are fewer of them, but when they do succeed, they make so much money that, in the words of the late Julia Phillips, the producer of *Jaws,* "there is no bottom line."

————

The City views everything as a business. This has always been true, and it lies at the heart of the fundamental dichotomy between it and industry: because although manufacturers, historically and to the present, have not been shy about wanting to be rich, they see the City's capital as a means to an end rather than as a master in itself. This has been a theme in British history for about two centuries, but the thing which changed under Margaret Thatcher was that for the first time the City now had unquestioned supremacy. It wasn't a debate anymore: what the City wanted, the City got. Manufacturing has declined precipitately in importance in the last three decades. Britain was once famous for its innovative approach to engineering and industry. No longer. The result was that what had once been a more or less balanced economy, with manufacturing and service sectors of comparable importance, now became one in which the financial sector was paramount.

Britain's banks were already big. Because of Britain's imperial and colonial history, its banks had a broad geographical spread: just as British Airways is, in the words of its own advertising, "the world's favourite airline" because of its proliferation of routes and destinations associated with the imperial past, so Britain's banks have long been international in their scope. In addition, we in Britain didn't have the wave of bank-taming legislation that America undertook in the 1930s, as a way of preventing a repeat of the Crash of 1929 and the ensuing Depression. The Glass-Steagall act was only the best known of a series of laws designed to limit the size and influence and, especially, the cross-state operation of the American banks. In Britain we never had a comparable set of laws targeting the size and activities of our banks. That was partly because we never had a moment of banker bashing to rival the one which took place during the Depression. The City's place in British life was never at risk from a populist backlash. Laws of this type were on the U.S. statute books well into the 1990s; but Britain had, thanks to the Big Bang, fully deregulated the operation of its banks by halfway through the previous decade. Our banks could take part in more or less any type of activity they wanted: investment banking (or "merchant banking," as it used to be called), securitization, retail banking directed at consumers, derivatives trading, you name it. Deregulated and opened to influxes of international capital, our banks grew bigger and bigger, along with the rest of our financial services industry. This was now the biggest and most important sector of our economy and was one of the few areas of British life which had a claim to dominate the world in its sector. (The whole question of what Britain is best at, in global terms, is an interesting one. There are four sectors in which Britain is world-class: finance, arms manufacturing, the creative arts, and higher education. Of these, the first receive strong government support, the second receive lavish investment and strong support, the third is largely left to mind its own business, and the fourth has been gradually run down, with three decades of consistent discouragement and underfunding. What would Britain look like today if instead of the arms industry or the City it had been our Russell Group universities which had been the subject of attempts to achieve world supremacy?)

The City of London, with its historic head start, and thanks to Big Bang another head start—in terms of the deregulatory boom of the 1980s—became a, or arguably the, global center of the new financial expansion. The derivatives market about which I've written, for instance, has its global headquarters in London: the average turnover of over-the-counter derivatives in London—remember, those are the ones directly traded between two counterparties, with no exchange or regulator in the middle—peaked in 2007 at a value of $2.105 trillion *every day*. That's right: every day. The figure for the total U.S. derivatives market was $959 billion. The AIG unit that wrote all the CDS policies which were to eventually destroy the company was based in London. The head of the unit, Joseph Cassano, earned $280 million in eight years running the operation, which despite its U.K. base seems not to have been regulated by our own FSA, because of a technical issue to do with its being a subsidiary of a U.S. company.[15] Here again we have the curse of the nonbank banks: a crucially important piece of global financial architecture which fell through regulatory cracks because the legislation had lagged so far behind the moneymen that the existing rules didn't apply to them. It was like the moment when William Webb Ellis picked up a ball, began to run with it, and in the process invented the game of rugby—except in this instance, the people watching the game stood around scratching their heads for a decade or so while a multitrillion-dollar market grew in front of them. That is where the culture of deregulation, and of ignored funny smells, took us: to a single unit of a single company being able to take the global financial system to the edge of destruction, and all without the attention of any regulator at all.

That brings us to the most important funny smell, and the most important counterfactual, of all. The credit crunch was based on a climate (the post–Cold War victory party of free-market capitalism), a problem (the subprime mort-gages), a mistake (the mathematical models of risk), and a failure (that of the regulators). It was the regulators' job to prevent both the collapse of individual companies and the systemic risks which ensued; they failed. But that failure wasn't due so much to the absence of attention to individual details as it was to an entire culture of the primacy of business, of money, of deregulation, of putting the interests of the financial sector first. This brought us to a point in which a belief in the free market became a kind of secular religion. The tenets of that religion are familiar, and they have been a central part of the story so far: the primacy of laissez-faire capitalism, the magically self-regulating nature of the market, the superiority of the free market to all other forms of human organization. These are all debatable, con-testable positions—but in the Anglo-Saxon world, we for-got to contest them. This should be an enduring lesson of the crisis—an understanding that the rules governing the operating of markets were not handed down on stone tab-lets but made by human beings and are in constant need of revision, supervision, and active, imaginative enforcement. We can't afford to forget this point: human beings make markets. A general recognition of that fact, led by the eco-nomics profession and taken to heart by politicians, would be a step so important as to be almost worth what it has cost to be reminded of it.

I have people I count as friends who work in the City. We get on in all the ways in which people get on, but there is sometimes a moment in talking to them when you hit a kind of wall. It's usually to do with fundamental assump-tions based on the primacy of money and the nonreality of other schemes of value. You get a glimpse into this world-view when you look at the *Economist*. It is an excellent paper (a term it prefers to "magazine"), in particular full of good firsthand fact-finding. The first 80 percent of almost every article is full of fresh things. But every single piece, on every single subject, reaches the same conclusion. Whatever you're reading about, it turns out that the solution is the same: more liberalization, more competition, more free markets. However nuanced and original the details in the bulk of the piece, the answer is always the same; it makes the *Economist* like an algebraic formula in which the answer is always x.

Tom Wolfe's term for the people at the pinnacle of this system was "masters of the universe." That was meant to be heavily, stingingly ironic—but the masters of the universe seemed not to notice that. They still seem not to. There's a reason for that. For most adults, the sensation of being proved right is usually a complex and bittersweet one. You might have said that your brother-in-law would turn out to be a no-goodnik, or that the forty-third president would turn out to be the worst in American history, and you may regard subsequent events as inarguable proof that you were right—but it's not an especially happy feeling. It changes nothing about the world outside your head. You were right. Congratulations. And? One of the peculiar things about the world of finance is that it freely offers the sensation of being proved right to its participants. Every transaction in the markets has a buyer and a seller, and in most cases one of them is right and the other wrong, because the price goes either up or down. The cumulative weight of this rightness-or-wrongness is one of the things that make financial types psychologically distinctive. Artists, sportsmen, surgeons, plumbers, and the rest of us have secret voices of doubt, inner reservations about ourselves, but if you go to work with money and make money, you can be proved right in the most inhumanly pure way. This is why people who have succeeded in the world of money tend to have such a high opinion of themselves. And this is why they seem to regard themselves as paragons of rationality, while others often regard them as slightly nuts. Outsiders don't often get a good look at this mind-set in its full pomp, but when we do, it makes an unforgettable impression. A couple of the best recent examples have come from the heads of imploded banks. The chairman and CEO of Lehman Brothers, Richard Fuld, in his no-apologies testimony to a congressional committee was one example. Another was the behavior of Sir Fred Goodwin after the meltdown and public rescue of RBS, when he claimed a pension of astonishing amplitude; astonishing not by the standard of banker pensions but by the standard of a failed company whose liabilities had been taken on by taxpayers.

These are just lurid examples of the insulating bubble of money and the comforting security of the cult. It wouldn't matter if it weren't for the fact that the psychology of the masters of the universe has played a vital role in our journey to this point. One of our culture's deepest beliefs is expressed in the question "If you're so smart, why ain't you rich?" But people in finance are rich—so it logically follows that everything they choose to do must be smart. That was the syllogism followed by too many people in the money business. The regulators failed; but they failed because the bankers made them fail. All the rules which existed, about bank capital and reserve requirements, about risk, and about cross-border regulatory supervision, were energetically, systematically, and determinedly circumvented by some of the banks. They treated the rules as things designed by thick people to slow them down and hamper their rightful profitability. It was self-evident to them that they had a better understanding of the risks they were taking than did anyone else. They behaved like drivers who regard speed limits as things to be obeyed only by muppets. It's as if they saw the thirty-miles-an-hour sign but then realized that the speed cameras wouldn't work if you were doing more than seventy—and took that as their cue to roar through built-up areas at the highest speed possible. The proliferation of nonbank banks, the pervasive use of derivatives to increase rather than to hedge risk, the overwhelming preference for over-the-counter derivatives, the use of off-balance-sheet vehicles—all of these things were critical contributors to the disaster, and all of them had, not just as some marginal benefit but as their central purpose, the determination to get around the banking rules. So, yes, the regulators were useless, but their failure wasn't like that of a lifeguard who doesn't notice that some of his swimmers are in trouble, it was that of a lifeguard supervising swimmers who are secretly pouring blood into the water because they think it would be more exciting if the place were livened up by a few sharks. Deregulation was a big part of this, and it should be borne in mind that every single one of the rule changes which paved the way for the crash was the result of energetic lobbying by the banks. When the banksters couldn't get the degree of deregulation they wanted, they went around the rules anyway. "Irresponsible": that's a word President Obama has used several times about the actions of the bankers. It's a good word.

It should also be said that it doesn't apply to all bankers. People in the City deeply resent the way they've all been associated with the actions of the (as they see it) relatively small number of people involved in the shenanigans which led to the credit crunch. Most of them don't trade asset-backed securities or work for off-balance-sheet subsidiaries, and they don't see why they are the target of such generalized anger and recrimination. There is truth in that, but there is also a failure to admit that this was a cultural issue, not just the result of a set of specific actions. In fact, the bankers have been careful not to show quite how much they've minded being the target of such generalized opprobrium. The damage done by people such as Richard Fuld and Sir Fred Goodwin is caused by the fact that they don't seem atypical; they seem not to feel any sense of responsibility for what's gone wrong, or that the rewards they earned during the good years were disproportionate. Mervyn King, the governor of the Bank of England, did not cover himself in kudos during the implosion of Northern Rock, but he now seems to have grasped this fundamental point about where we are. "The cost of this crisis," he told an audience of City bigwigs at the Mansion House, the definitive annual bankers' shindig, in 2009, "is not to be measured simply in terms of its impact on public finances, the destruction of wealth and the number of jobs lost. They are also to be seen in the lost trust in the financial sector in other parts of our economy. . . . 'My word is my bond' are old words. 'My word is my CDO-squared' will never catch on."

He gets it—belatedly, perhaps, but he does get it. Many of his colleagues in the City seem not to. What bankers will sometimes do, preferably sotto voce and in private, is mutter something along the lines of "the incentives were wrong." To civilians, that might seem a way of admitting that bankers paid themselves too much. But that isn't what they're saying. The problem with incentives was not the absolute levels of pay which the masters of the universe awarded themselves but the fact that their pay emphasized and encouraged the benefits of taking risks, while removing any of the consequences when things went wrong. The result was a system that, with hindsight, was certain to go wrong: if you encourage ever-greater levels of risk, you are sooner or later bound to have a blowup.

Part of this is laughably simple: bankers' pay structures rewarded them when things went up but did not punish them when things went down. That, added to the fact that so much pay came in the form of bonuses, encouraged a culture of gambling on big returns in good years. The good years were total bonanzas. As for the bad years, the bankers didn't have to pay any money back; they were so well paid that there was in effect no downside.

There was one other, hugely important additional factor. The banks had a reason for thinking there was no downside to their risks. I've already said that the banks were TBTF, too big to fail, and that this will have enormous consequences for all of us over the next decade or decades. But TBTF also helped us arrive in the place we're in now by creating a further lopsidedness in the incentive structure of the banking industry. The banks knew that however bad and big a hole they got into, it would be impossible for governments not to help them out of it; which meant that they could carry on taking big bets, safely knowing that if the bets went bad, their respective governments—which means us, the taxpayers—would pick up the tab. Imagine if you go to a casino and play roulette, and every time you win, you keep all the money. But whenever the wheel lands on zero, you lose a sum amounting to ten times all the money you have won to date—and the good news is, you don't have to pay it: the government steps in and picks up the tab, and you keep your previous winnings. How cool is that? In this system, your only incentive is to keep making bigger and bigger bets and making more and more money.

So "incentive" sounds like nerdspeak and bankerspeak,

but it in fact describes a critically important funny smell. Misaligned incentives were so much part of the culture that even the most glaring, blatant, reeking examples seemed normal to all participants. The biggest of them, and the one with the worst consequences, concerned the bond-rating agencies. I've already mentioned these bodies. They award the ratings, which have a critical effect on the way all sorts of institutions and debts are regarded; they affect both specific bonds and also the companies and governments which issue them. In the words of the *New York Times* columnist Thomas Friedman, "There are two superpowers in the world today in my opinion. There's the United States and there's Moody's Bond Rating Service. The United States can destroy you by dropping bombs, and Moody's can destroy you by downgrading your bonds. And believe me, it's not clear sometimes who's more powerful." [16]

The highest grade of debt, AAA, is supposed to be as safe as U.S. government T-bills; in other words, it's the safest debt in the world and represents the rate of return an investor can expect for zero risk. It's even safer than houses, because house prices go up and down; it's safer than sticking your money under the mattress, because you might get burgled or your house might burn down. The status of AAA-grade debt is written into various statutes; many publicly regulated bodies aren't allowed to invest in anything of lower grade than AAA. In other cases, institutions are legally prevented from investing in anything below BBB-grade debt, so-called junk bonds. The ratings agencies' verdicts are so taken as holy writ that they are incorporated into the Basel rules on bank reserves.

When governments lose AAA status for their debt, it is both an embarrassment and a potential disaster, because that means it's going to be more expensive for them to raise money in the future. For instance, Britain this year is borrowing £175 billion from the markets; if it were to lose its AAA rating—and it's already on the "watch list" of the ratings agency S&P, giving us a yellow card warning—future borrowing would cost us a lot more, because we would have to pay higher interest rates to attract lenders. There have even been early, tentative mutterings about the AAA status of U.S. government debt. For the United States to lose its AAA rating would be an event so unprecedented that no one can even guess what the consequences would be, but it's safe to say it would resemble the alien in *The Thing*: "I don't know what it is, but it's big, it's weird, and it's mighty pissed off."

Given how important the ratings agencies are, with the power quite literally to shape the destiny of entire nations, one might expect there to have been strict rules circumscribing their behavior, their rulings, and any influences which could be brought to bear on them. But in fact the ratings agencies had the world's worst case of misaligned incentives. Their main clients—the people who most depended on them for their ratings—were the banks and other investors who traded and bought bonds based on the ratings agencies' assessments. Once upon a time, these investors had access to the agencies' ratings by way of a subscription service, but by the mid-1970s the SEC changed its view of how the business should work, having apparently decided that the ratings were too important to be a restricted, subscription-based service and instead were something that the broader community had a right to know. The ratings still had to be paid for, of course, so the SEC decreed that from then on the company issuing the bond should pay the ratings agency for its assessment, which would then be a matter of public knowledge. This immediately created a conflict of interest. The SEC, acting from unimpeachable motives, had accidentally set up a situation in which the people who were being graded by the ratings agencies were simultaneously the ratings agencies' main paymasters. The process of assessing bonds and debt instruments is a very, very big business.

Historically, the ratings agencies had mostly been involved in the business of assessing corporate bonds. That changed. From about 2001, when the housing market, and then the mortgage-backed securities market, and then the subprime mortgage-backed securities market all took off, the ratings agencies were increasingly in the business of assessing mortgage-backed securities. These were very lucrative. The assessment of a standard package of mortgage-backed securities paid the ratings agencies three times more than did that of a standard corporate bond.[17] Talk about misaligned incentives! The ratings agencies were paid according to volume, so the more business they did, the more they got paid; they were yet another component of the subprime chain which basically didn't care whether or not people could actually afford to repay their loans. And they were yet another component of the subprime chain whose business boomed. Between 2002 and 2006, Moody's revenue doubled, and its share price tripled.[18] What the companies issuing the securities wanted was AAA ratings, and with the assistance of the ratings agencies—not just in terms of published models but sometimes with actual hands-on help in designing the debt—that's what they got. The end result was that almost 90 percent of the mortgage-backed CDOs were assessed as AAA grade. Very little corporate debt is rated AAA, but the entire industry had now gone through the looking glass and persuaded itself of the magically secure status of the new CDO instruments; so we arrived in the bizarre position in which poor people struggling to pay back their mortgages had miraculously produced the world's most secure financial instruments. This was a fortunate conclusion to reach for both the banks, which made money issuing the CDOs, and the ratings agencies, which made money assessing them. The banks were not shy about saying that if an agency would not give them the rating they wanted, they would go shopping elsewhere. All this added up to create a situation in which the ratings agencies had no incentive to point out the weaknesses of CDOs and every incentive to shut up and rubber-stamp them.

All of this—all the funny smells, the missed warning signals, the misaligned incentives, the distorted attitudes to risk, the arrogance of the masters of the universe, the complicity of regulators, the doziness of legislators—symptomized a culture, and also constituted one. It was the culture of the financial industry. It didn't have to turn out like this. There are occasional frustrating glimpses of how things could have been different in both Britain and the United States. The common good and the interests of the financial industry are not identical—a fact that for the previous three decades has conveniently been forgotten. The financial culture could have been similar but the outcome different if it had not been for those failures of regulation and legislation; they were critical to allowing the culture to go too far and produce the credit crunch. We know that for sure because of the counterfactual example of a country which had a broadly similar Anglo-Saxon attitude to business yet did not go down the path of doctrinaire liberalization and laissez-faire when it came to legislating the financial industry: Canada. The OECD rates Canada's banks as the safest in the world—the United States comes fortieth, two places behind Botswana, and the United Kingdom comes forty-fourth. Canada is the only one of the G8 countries not to have bailed out its banks. The reason is that Canada didn't join the party. Its banks had higher capital requirements than elsewhere, the legacy in part of a scare about bank liquidity in the early 1990s which left Canada nurturing a realistic sense of the systemic risks, just at the point when other economies were yelling "Woo-hoo!" and tearing their regulatory clothes off. Other features of the Canadian banking system included lower levels of securitization and the use of securitization mainly as a way of increasing liquidity rather than as a tool for spreading the risks of CDS—and CDO-type instruments; very low levels of involvement in mortgage-backed securities; a law insisting that if anyone was borrowing more than 80 percent of the value of the home, he or she had to take out insurance on the debt; and no tax relief on mortgage interest. Most of all, it was a reluctance to join in the fiesta of laissez-faire, which no doubt owed a good deal to the Canadian national appetite for distinguishing itself from its hypercapitalist neighbor to the south. This, incidentally, did not come at the cost of falling behind in other areas: since 2004, Canadians' average incomes have grown at 11 percent a year, compared with 5 percent in the United States. A country doesn't have to have a frenetically overactive financial sector in order to have a thriving economy.

SEVEN

THE BILL

The last question is the one which, looking forward, is the most important: now what?

I've already mentioned my belief that the Western liberal democracies are the best societies that have ever existed—which isn't the same thing as saying that they are perfect. Citizens of those societies are, on aggregate, the most fortunate people who have ever lived. Almost everyone in the West lives a quality and length of life which would have been the envy of a pharaoh or a Roman emperor and which most of our ancestors, and most of the populations of the rest of the world, would swap for their own prospects in an eye blink. It's an amazing state of affairs—and one which, broadly speaking, was predicted by the greatest economist who ever lived, John Maynard Keynes, in an essay he wrote in 1930, "Economic Possibilities for our Grandchildren." He was writing in the immediate aftermath of the great Crash (which incidentally, in his capacity as an investor, cost him a packet), but he wasn't pessimistic; indeed, he thought the general contemporary climate of pessimism was overdone. Britain had got steadily richer for decades and was going to continue to do so. Keynes, entertainingly, pinpointed the initial cause of British prosperity as Sir Francis Drake's theft of gold from the Spanish in 1580. From her piece of that action, Queen Elizabeth was able to pay off all the country's foreign debts, balance the budget, and end up with about £40,000 left over: an amount which, at 3 percent compounded, added up in 1930 to the £4 billion which was Britain's foreign reserves. In terms of GDP per capita, Britain was four times richer than it had been when Drake stole the gold. In a century's time, by 2030, Keynes estimated, the country would be between four and eight times richer again, and this would mean that, in effect, mankind's greatest problem, the struggle for bare economic survival, would have been solved.

His prediction is on track—at least, it's on track economically. With twenty-one years to go to the deadline, we're already 4.6 times richer than we were in Keynes's day. But Keynes was deeply wrong about how that would affect us. He thought that we would realize how lucky we were. "When the accumulation of wealth is no longer of high social importance, there will be great changes in the code of morals. We shall be able to rid ourselves of many of the pseudo-moral principles which have hag-ridden us for two hundred years, by which we have exalted some of the most distasteful of human qualities into the position of the highest virtues." [1] He was talking about greed and acquisitiveness.

We shall be able to afford to dare to assess the money-motive at its true value. The love of money as a possession—as distinguished from the love of money as a means to the enjoyments and realities of life—will be recognised for what it is, a somewhat disgusting morbidity, one of those semi-criminal, semi-pathological propensities which one hands over with a shudder to the specialists in mental disorder. All kinds of social customs and economic practices, affecting the distribution of wealth and economic rewards and penalties, which we now maintain at all costs, however distasteful and unjust they may be in themselves, because they are tremendously useful in promoting the accumulation of capital, we shall then be free, at last, to discard.

He thought that the overridingly important issue in this world would be how to live and how to learn from "the delightful people who are capable of taking direct enjoyment of things, the lilies of the field who toil not, neither do they spin."

Keynes sure was wrong about all that. The great increase in our prosperity over the last decades has caused no general sense that we should now slow down and reflect on where we are, who we are, and what we want from life. That is particularly apparent right here, right now, in 2010. Sometimes when you're on a journey, your arrival at a particular destination completely changes your sense of what happened to you on the way. Looking back, you realize that some of the time you were lost and didn't know it, and some of the time you were on the right track and didn't know it, and perhaps you also think that the journey wasn't worthwhile or that you would have done the whole thing differently if you had known then what you know now.

That's the point we've now arrived at, at the end of the new millennium's first decade, in the aftermath of the credit crunch. This is the spot from which we look back and realize where we've been and decide what to make of it. Looking back, it turns out that we've just lived through an economic golden age. It turned out to be a fake golden age, one based on debt and on an unsustainable credit bubble and underpinned by a financial system which was, it turned out, taking crazily miscalculated risks—but we didn't know that at the time. In fact, most of us had no idea it was a golden age; we didn't know that we were living through what for many of us will turn out to be the best economic times of our lives. I wish someone had told us: I wish someone had had the nerve to do what Harold Macmillan was roundly denounced for doing in 1957, gone on TV to tell us that we'd never had it so good. At least we'd have had a reference point, something to disagree with and force us to think about the boom we were living through. Would we have spent quite so much time pigging out on cheap credit? Would we have been quite so unreflecting, so spendthrift, so greedy? This is one of the many ways in which Iceland is an example to or forerunner of other countries caught up in the crisis. The Icelandic cab driver who told me that "it was thirty or forty people who did this, and the rest of us who are having to pay" was telling the truth: it was indeed, in Iceland and elsewhere, a tiny minority of people directly responsible for the financial shenanigans behind the crash. And it is indeed everyone else who is having to pick up the bill. But there is a missing component there, and it is the fact that so many of us were caught up in the good times when they were rolling.

Credit bubbles and asset bubbles don't just happen without people joining in them, borrowing and spending more, betting on asset prices going upward and the suspension of the never-untrue, never-popular rule that what goes up must come down. One thing lacking in the public discourse about the crisis is someone to point out the extent to which we helped do this to ourselves, because we allowed our governments to do it and because we were greedy and stupid. It's not just bankers who have been indulging in greed, short-termism, and fantasy economics. In addition to our stretched mortgage borrowing, Britain has half of the total European credit card debt. The industry did everything it could to egg us on, but that is still a horrible fact—and although it's nice to reserve the blame for banks who made lending too easy, the great British public is just as much to blame. We grew obsessed with the price of our houses, felt richer than we should, borrowed money we didn't have, spent it on junk, and now that the downturn has happened—as it was bound to do—we want someone else to blame. Well boo hoo. Bankers are to blame, but we're to blame too. That's just as well, because we're the ones who are going to have to pay.

Margaret Thatcher began, and Labour continued, a switch toward an economy which was reliant on financial services, at the expense of other areas of society. One can argue (and I would argue) with that, but what was equally damaging for Britain was the hegemony of economic, or quasi-economic, thinking. The economic metaphor came to be applied to every aspect of modern life, especially the areas in which it simply didn't belong. In fields such as education, equality of opportunity, health care, employees' rights, the social contract, and culture, the first conversation to happen should be about values and principles; then you have the conversation about costs and what you as a society can afford. In Britain in the last twenty to thirty years that has all been the wrong way round. There was a kind of reverse takeover, in which City values came to dominate

the whole of British life. There needs to be a general acceptance that the model has failed: the brakes-off, deregulate
or die, privatize or stagnate, lunch is for wimps, greed is
good, what's good for the financial sector is good for the
economy model; the "sack the bottom 10 percent," bonus-
driven, "if you can't measure it, it isn't real" model; the
model which spread from the City to government and from
there through the whole culture, in which the idea of value
has gradually faded to be replaced by the idea of price.

When the credit crunch first began—after the initial
waves of panic and the moment when "this sucker could
go down"—I thought that there might be a general reevalu-
ation of where we all were. We wouldn't notice and reflect
just on the past decade of good times but on the whole
question of what our societies had as their goals, where
capitalism had brought us, and whether we wanted to keep
working quite as hard as we had, in the direction of an
always-receding vision of contentment. The "hedonic tread-
mill" is what this is called: as you have more and more,
your idea of what it would take to be happy keeps receding
just out of reach. It's always the next pay raise, the next
purchase, the next place you move to or go on holiday
which will make you happy. The credit crunch could have
been a moment to reflect on that. We in the West can do
something that no people in history have done: we can
show the world that we know when we have enough. As
the planet runs out of resources, due mainly to the fact that
everyone on it wants to live a lifestyle equivalent to those
of us in the West, this lesson would have the potential to
save the world.

I don't think this moment of realization is going to happen. That's mainly because although we might be rich by
global and historical standards, we don't feel it; and even

when our livelihoods aren't at risk from the recession and the general slowdown, we are all about to feel significantly poorer. That's because we're about to get the bill. In the course of this book I have a few times laid out things which are bleeding obvious to people in the world of finance and virtually unknown to those outside. Here's one of them: that the recovery everyone is longing for is the point when we will get the bill. It's when we recover that we will start to pay back the cost of what happened. Governments can't begin to fix the holes in their own balance sheets—holes which get rapidly worse as tax revenues collapse and spending vooms upward—until the economy is growing again. Up until then, the economy is too delicate for the state to get out its trowel and begin to extract the increased taxes it's going to need. The appearance of the famous "green shoots" and the return to economic growth which follows them is merely the moment at which we catch the waiter's eye and make the waggling mime to indicate it's time to pay.

And it's going to be one hell of a bill. For the sheer size of the Figures of Doom, nothing can beat the world's biggest economy, which has had a property bubble, a credit bubble, and years of growing deficit thanks to George W. Bush's high-spirited experiment in big-spending conservatism. The projected deficit—this is based on the government's own figures—will come to $7.14 trillion over the next ten years. As for the bailouts, there are various ways of calculating their cost so far, with Neil Barofsky, the special inspector general in charge of administering the program, putting the cost as of March 31, 2009, at $2.98 trillion.[2] By adding to that the imminent bailout of the gigantic financial corporation Citigroup, the market commentator Barry Ritholtz came up with a total cost of the bailout as $4.6165 trillion.[3] (He also makes the point that some estimates of the cost are even higher, quoting a Bloomberg figure of $7.76 trillion.) He then put the figure into historical perspective. That number is bigger than the Marshall Plan, the Louisiana Purchase, the Apollo moon landings, the 1980s savings and loan crisis, the Korean War, the New Deal, the invasion of Iraq, the Vietnam War, and the total cost of NASA's space flights, all added together— repeat, *added together* (and yes, the old figures are adjusted upward for inflation).

Not that we in the United Kingdom are any better off. The 30 percent decline in the value of the pound is unlikely to go away as quickly as it arrived. The reason the pound has crashed is simple: the markets are pricing in the fact that we the taxpayer are on the hook for the losses made by our banks. The markets assume that we can't or won't default on our government debt—that would mean we simply can't afford to pay back the amount we're currently borrowing. They're probably right about that. But Alistair Darling's desperately grim budget of 2009 made it clear just how deep in the mire we are. As for how bad it is and how quickly it's gone bad, well: in April 2008, at the time of the budget, the projected deficit for 2009–10 was £38 billion. By November 24, the projected deficit was £118 billion. At the budget on April 22, 2009, Darling admitted that the real figure is going to be £175 billion. The total projected borrowing for the next four years is £606 billion. National debt will hit 79 percent of GDP—the highest peacetime figure ever. The economy is going to have its worst year since 1945. The debt is going to cost from £35 to £47 billion a year to service—that's just the debt alone. We'll be spending more on debt than on the entire transport budget. All this means tax raises, a near-total freeze on government spending, massive public-sector job cuts, companies laying off every worker they can to save costs, and in turn a dramatic upward spike in unemployment. The one easy thing the government might be able to do to help itself is to make inflation go up—that would help because it would decrease the real cost of the debt. An inflation rate of 5 percent would means that the debt would go down in cost by 5 percent every year, magically and just by itself. From the point of view of a heavily indebted government, that's good news; for other parts of the economy—for borrowers and anyone holding sterling—not so much. Then, to try to bring the inflation under control, the government would raise interest rates, which would slow the economy and cost jobs, and we'd be back where we were in the early 1980s, with high interest rates, high inflation, high unemployment, the government wielding an ax on public expenditure, and a bitterly divided polity, one in which the interests of everybody on the state's payroll (both those on benefits and those on state-derived employment) are in direct conflict with those of everybody else.

To compound this already desperate picture, we also have a huge level of personal debt, arising directly from our credit bubble. The average British household owes 160 percent of its annual income. That makes us, individually and collectively, a lot like the cartoon character who's run off the end of a cliff and hasn't realized it yet. In January 2009, the investor-pundit Jim Rogers advised anyone listening to "sell any sterling you might have. It's finished. I hate to say it, but I would not put any money in the UK."[4] That wasn't nice or polite, but it put into the public domain what a lot of international moneymen are saying in private. More

to the point, it's a policy on which they have already acted.
So roads and schools and hospitals will go unbuilt and un-
repaired, medical treatments will go unbought, nurses and
policemen and council workers will be laid off. Six hundred thousand jobs have been created in local government
in the last few years. Most of them will have to go. And
then there's the really gigantic argument over the public-
service pensions, which are paid for out of current tax re-
ceipts. I don't know anyone who has studied this problem
who thinks that the government will be able to afford them.
Can you imagine the fights that are going to happen? The
political polarization between public and private-sector employees, the savagery of the cuts, the bitterness of the arguments, the furious sense of righteousness on both sides? It'll
be Thatcher all over again, and the current period of mana-
gerial nonpolitics will seem as distant as Clement Attlee's
creation of the welfare state.

That's because we in Britain are, to use a technical economic term, screwed. Economies around the world are
struggling. Because nobody is spending money, even relatively blameless countries such as Germany, with low levels
of debt and workforces which actually make things, are
having a difficult time. Germany's economy was predicted
to contract by 5.4 percent in 2009. A banker explained it
like this: "When your country's economy depends on people buying a car every three years and they decide that
they'll only buy a car every five years, you're finished. Off a
cliff." Something similar goes for Spain, where the end of
the property boom has caused a spike in unemployment to
17.4 percent, almost doubling in a year, or Ireland, which
has contracted by a truly horrendous 8 percent and where

people have gone from owning private helicopters to losing their homes in six months flat. All of those countries are in trouble. But there are four things you don't want to have, going into the current crisis. (1) You don't want to have had a boom based on a property bubble. (2) You don't want to have a consumer credit bubble. (3) You don't want to have an economy based on financial services. (4) You don't want your government to have just gone on a massive spending spree. We in the United Kingdom have all four of those things that you don't want.

What this will lead to, I think, is more anger. Again, Iceland is the forerunner: there, the incumbent government's obliviousness to the consequences of its own policies eventually triggered the "pots and pans revolution," in which people banged kitchenware outside the Parliament building until the government quit and called an election. As the bill is paid, and especially as taxes go up while services and jobs go away, people are going to get steadily and inexorably more furious. I'm not sure at whom; I hope it's at the responsible bodies, but I wouldn't bet on it. Public rage is like lightning and tends to discharge its energies at anyone who has the bad luck to be prominent in the wrong way at the wrong time.

As for where the anger would go if it were properly directed, that's easy to answer: at the banks and at the governments which let the banks do what they did. The evidence on this count isn't yet in, because the all-important question isn't what legislation is debated and white-papered but what gets put on the statute book, and also how the laws are enforced—since, as I've argued, the regime is as important as the framework. At the moment the atmosphere is thick with proposals, many of them ingenious and timely: for instance, the Obama administration's plan to force securitizers to retain a proportion of the risks on their own books, rather than to sell all of it—now, that's an excellent idea, even if the touted share of the risk to be retained is probably set too low at 5 percent. Laws on forcing the banks to have "countercyclical" reserve levels are a good idea too; the idea is that banks will have to put aside more cash in boom times, to be prepared for the subsequent busts. Measures bringing the nonbank "banks" and financial intermediaries into the legislative net aren't just obviously necessary, they're twenty years overdue. Laws targeting mistaken bonuses and incentives and allowing for the possibility of "clawback" if bonuses are paid for actions which are later exposed as mistaken are also a good idea. The Tories, who have taken full benefit for being out of office during the bust (even though it's 100 percent certain that they wouldn't have done anything different if they had been in power), have been much firmer than the government in advocating policies designed to separate commercial banking from retail banking—splitting the casino from the piggy bank. The idea is that customer-oriented deposit-holding banks should be guaranteed by the state and tightly regulated, whereas the boys-will-be-boys willy-wagging masters of the universe should be free to play their games in investment banks which can freely implode at no cost to the taxpayer.

There are two schools of thought about that idea. School 1: It is an indispensable step to restoring the financial sector, and the wider economy, to health. School 2: It wouldn't work. I subscribe to school 1, but school 2 has some strong arguments, among them that modern financial operations are so tightly interlinked that it simply isn't possible to keep them clean and clear in the manner envisioned. Also, School 2 points to the failure of some "narrow

banks," as they're called, in the current crisis. The answer
to that point is that the banks weren't as narrow as all that
and that the systemic crisis was already so far advanced
that all bets were off. School 2, however, has another, even
stronger argument, which is that the idea that huge investment banks would be allowed to fail is not, in practice,
true. In the event of a crisis for a company such as, say,
Goldman Sachs, a government bailout would be arranged,
whatever the rhetoric had been, because the lesson of
Lehman's collapse was that "too big to fail" is a reality. It
would be lovely if that weren't true, but the unfortunate
fact is that when one of these big banks went down, it
nearly took the global financial system with it; so we won't
be trying that again, thanks. Nobody wants to dwell on
this fact, because it is such an uncomfortable one for bankers and politicians alike—not to mention for the taxpayers
who paid for the last set of bailouts and will have to pay
for the next lot too, if and when the banks blow up again.
We are nowhere near what is desperately needed, a set of
arrangements whereby banks can fail in an orderly way. We
need to create a system by which banks can fail without
bringing one another down; by which they can go into administration and have their affairs unwound in the same
way that ordinary businesses do. I have yet to see anybody
come up with credible propsals to do that.

So I accept School 2's argument that these institutions
will not be allowed to fail in current circumstances, but I
think this point can be substantially fixed, with another
change to the law. The change should be that if a bank
(broadly defined) receives any taxpayer money, the existing
shareholders are (broadly speaking) wiped out. That's what
happens to investors in other institutions: if the firm you've
bought a share in goes broke, you lose your money. At the

moment, that doesn't happen with banks because of the TBTF problem, which means that shareholders, and their representatives on bank boards, need only have to talk the talk about managing risk. This simple and brutal change in the law would make it incumbent on them to make sure the companies they own stay comfortably on the safe side of the street when it comes to managing their risks, and if that means smaller profits, well, that's better than being wiped out completely. Go and ask the Enron employees who had all their pensions invested in the company's stock. Without a change along these lines, there is no reason to think that something very like the credit crunch couldn't happen again.

That's because all the laws can address is what's legal. They can't stretch deep into banking and change its culture; the problem is that that's what most needs to be changed. The power and complexity of modern financial instruments combine with the will to profit and the reality of TBTF to create a situation in which, as soon as the rules are made, people will be looking for ways around them. Not all bankers, obviously—not even a majority of them, nowhere near. But there will always be someone who wants to try cheating the thirty-mile-an-hour speed camera by driving at more than seventy. In this case, much of the rule evading will involve differences between national legislation about banks. Some countries will always try to seek a competitive advantage by having looser banking laws; some banks will always try to exploit that fact. This story has made it clear, I hope, that finance is completely transnational in nature: national frontiers are there purely as things to be exploited, via their differing legislation.

This, again, is to do with culture. The counterexamples to banking can be found in industries such as health care: doctors don't, for the most part, pride themselves on saying

"What the hell, nobody's looking, so I'm just going to re-use this dirty needle." An even stronger counter example is aviation. I am terrified of flying, but even I have to admit that airlines have been extraordinarily effective at generat-ing a culture of safety, in which that value is unquestionedly paramount. This is allied with an impressive degree of transparency—impressive, verging on outright scary, in the case of the United States, where anyone can look up the service record of any aircraft, from a laptop at the airport, just before getting on board. That is partly because the in-dustry has learnt, in the words of easyJet's founder, Stelios Haji-Ioannou (who learnt this lesson in the oil tanker busi-ness): "If you think safety is expensive, try having an acci-dent." But the culture of modern banking is not like that; in fact, it's close to the opposite of that. The bankers' slo-gan is something closer to "We're not that fussed about safety, because if we have an accident, it's you who pays." There are already clear signs that for some banks the party is back on. From the *Financial Times* in July 2009, at a time when some banks such as RBS, Merrill Lynch, and Citigroup were still deep in the mire: "thriving rivals— JPMorgan, Goldman Sachs, Morgan Stanley, Barclays, Deutsche Bank and Credit Suisse—are talking privately of a record second quarter. They have benefited from lively markets for commodity and foreign exchange trading, at profit margins that are between two and eight times higher than before the height of the financial crisis last autumn. . . . 'There used to be 15 banks competing. Now there are six,' says one investment banker. 'This is a phenomenal en-vironment. I've never seen anything like this in 20 years in the business.' " In other words, the credit crunch has cre-ated never-better trading conditions—for the banks. Gold-man Sachs is the most spectacular example of this. That

bank went from having to end its status as an investment
bank and take federal support, in September 2008, to de-
claring all-time record profits—with bonuses to match—in
July 2009. The bank, which would have gone under without government help and had to borrow $10 billion from
the taxpayer, was eight months later setting aside $11.8 bil-
lion in pay, bonuses, and benefits for itself. That is obscene.
The incentives—and disincentives—need to be fixed, and in
short order. The big club of potential nationalization needs
to be taken out and brandished warningly.

Will this happen? I shouldn't think so. The U.K. and
U.S. plans are different, but at their heart they both show
the governments going to almost unbelievable lengths in
order to avoid taking the troubled banks into public ownership or to fully transfer the risks to where they belong—
with the shareholders. Our governments are prepared to
pay for them but not to force their owners to bear the full
burden of their risks.

There are four reasons for the reluctance to use nationalization as a threat, of which the first isn't a real reason
but a piece of political guff.

1. Because the government would be bad at it. This
   is the only reason governments are willing to give
   in public, and it fails the most elementary test of
   all: only a professional politician can say it with a
   straight face. Bad at running the banks compared
   to the bankers who broke capitalism? Please. But
   this is the closest they can get to admitting the first
   real reason, which is:

2. Because if the banks were taken over, then every
   decision they made would come at a potential political cost to the government. Your state-owned

mortgage lender is threatening to repossess your house after you fell behind on the payments? Blame the government. Your firm is laying off half its workforce because the bank won't roll over its loan? Blame the government. This, of course, is in addition to all the other economic things for which people are already blaming the government. People are already grumbling but to nowhere the extent they would if the banks were directly owned by the state. Politicians simply aren't willing to take on the responsibility for the banks' actions.

3. They also don't want to admit the extent to which we are all now liable for the losses made by the banks. Guess what, though: it's too late.

The fourth and deepest reason why the government won't nationalize the banks is:

4. Because it would be so embarrassing. Some of the embarrassment is superficial: on the not-remembering-somebody's-name-at-a-social-occasion level. The Anglo-Saxon economies have had decades of boom mixed with what now seem, in retrospect, smallish periods of downturn. During that they/we have shamelessly lectured the rest of the world on how they should be running their economies. We've gloated at the French fear of debt, laughed at the Germans' nineteenth-century emphasis on manufacturing, told the Japanese that they can't expect to get over their "lost decade" until they kill their zombie banks, and so on. It's embarrassing to be in a worse condition than all of them.

There is, however, a deeper embarrassment, one which verges on a form of psychological or ideological crisis. The huge bailouts of major financial institutions means that the Anglo-Saxon model of capitalism has failed. The level of state intervention in the United States and United Kingdom at this moment is at a level comparable to that of wartime. We have, in effect, had to declare war to get us out of the hole created by our economic system. We have been left with these grotesque hybrids, privately owned banks which are able to generate boggling profits because their risks are underwritten by the taxpayer. It is a 100 percent pure form of socialism for the rich. There is no model or precedent for this, and no way to argue that it's all right really, because under such-and-such a model of capitalism . . . there is no such model. It just isn't supposed to work like this, and there is no road map for what's happened. It's for that reason that the thing the governments least want to do—take over the banks—is something that needs to be prepared for, not just for economic reasons but for ethical ones too.

So: a huge, unregulated boom in which almost all the upside went directly into private hands, followed by a gigantic bust in which the losses were socialized. That is literally nobody's idea of how the world is supposed to work. It is just as much an abomination to the free marketeer as it is to the social democrat or outright leftist. But the models and alternatives don't seem to be forthcoming: there is an ideological and theoretical vacuum where the challenge from the Left used to be. Capitalism no longer has a global antagonist, just at the moment when it has never needed one more. Or rather, capitalism has found a deadly opponent, but the problem is that the opponent is capitalism itself. The last eleven years have seen the Long-Term Capital Management debacle, an unprecedented system-threatening implosion generated by flawed mathematical models; the Enron collapse, the unprecedented exposure of a huge and hugely respected company as being, in its very essence, an accounting fraud; and now the credit crunch, an unprecedented self-generated financial implosion. The evidence has to be that these scares are getting bigger and faster and happening closer together—and that must be a logical conclusion, given that it describes a simple reality about the bigger, faster global movement of capital. Why wouldn't the nasty turns have got bigger? Everything else has. The trouble is that the Western world, and the world at large, cannot afford another bust like the current one—not now and probably not for a generation to come.

About twenty years ago, the visionary climate scientist James Lovelock said that what the earth needed was the equivalent of a small heart attack. He said that the effect of such an episode is, in individuals' lives, often beneficial, because it forces them to face the facts about themselves and to adopt a healthier lifestyle. The planet needed something like that to get humanity's attention for what we have been doing to it. The earth didn't get its small heart attack, but the credit crunch is capitalism's equivalent. It's the point at which we all have a chance to take a look at ourselves, our banking systems, and our politicians and make some changes. On the political level, we have the chance to insist that our governments change the rules to make sure that this truly can't happen again—because if there is even the sliver of a chance that it can, it will; that's the nature of modern markets. Otherwise, we'll be doing the equivalent of discharging ourselves from hospital after that small heart attack and going straight out to celebrate with a carton of Rothmans, a bottle of tequila, and a supersized Big Mac with jumbo fries. Free-market capitalism's victory party lasted for two decades: now it's time to slow down, calm down, and decide how to make the finance industry back into something which serves the rest of society, rather than preying on it. And the level of our individual response is just as important. On that level, we have to start thinking about when we have sufficient—sufficient money, sufficient stuff—and whether we really need the things we think we do, beyond what we already have. In a world running out of resources, the most important ethical, political, and ecological idea can be summed up in one simple word: "enough."

ACKNOWLEDGMENTS

Mary-Kay Wilmers was the onlie begetter of this book. It was her idea for me to write about banks in the *London Review of Books* which got me started, and her subsequent suggestions for follow-up pieces which kept me going. This book wouldn't exist without her and the *LRB*. I'm grateful to her and her colleagues for all their editorial work.

Henry Finder at *The New Yorker* has been his usual distinctive mixture of brilliance and calm. I have been helped immeasurably by his commissioning and his editorial advice.

I am grateful to Lidija Hass for her invaluable sleuthing help.

I would particularly like to thank Sara Stefánsdottír for her assistance in Reykjavík. In Iceland I would also like to thank Rakel Stefánsdottír, Valgarður Bragason, Snorri Jónnson, Kári Sturluson, Helga Vala and Daði Ingólfsson.

In Baltimore, I'd especially like to thank Steve Hunter and Jean Marbella for their hospitality and advice. I'd also like to thank Ann LoLordo, Fern Shen, Lisa Evans, Mary Waldrow, Tony Damazio, and Philip Robinson.

I would also like to thank Fram Dinshaw, Rhomaios Ram, Nicolas Doisy, and Richard Smith.

———

I would like to thank *The Atlantic* for permission to quote Simon Johnson's article "The Quiet Coup," and the Nobel Foundation for permission to quote Daniel Kahneman's Biography.

SOURCES

This is a list both of sources and of suggestions for further reading. These are all books from which I have learnt a great deal.

Ahamed, Liaquat. *Lords of Finance: The Bankers Who Broke the World*. Penguin Press, New York, 2009.

Akerlof, George, and Robert Shiller. *Animal Spirits: How Human Psychology Drives the Economy, and Why It Matters for Global Capitalism*. Princeton, Princeton, 2009.

Bernstein, Peter. *Against the Gods: The Remarkable Story of Risk*. Wiley, New York, 1998.

Bitner, Richard. *Confessions of a Subprime Lender: An Insider's Tale of Greed, Fraud, and Ignorance*. Wiley, New York, 2008.

Buchan, James. *Frozen Desire*. Picador, London, 1996.

Buffett, Warren, and Lawrence A. Cunningham. *The Essays of Warren Buffett: Lessons for Corporate America*. 1998.

Coggan, Philip. *The Money Machine: How the City Works.* Penguin, London, 2002.

Cohan, William D. *House of Cards: How Wall Street's Gamblers Broke Capitalism.* Doubleday, New York, 2009.

Einhorn, David. *Fooling Some of the People All of the Time.* Wiley, Hoboken, 2008.

Ferguson, Niall. *The Ascent of Money: A Financial History of the World.* Penguin Press, London, 2008.

Keynes, John Maynard. *The General Theory of Employment, Interest and Money.* Cambrige University Press, Cambridge, U.K., 2008.

Kindleberger, Charles P., and Robert Z. Aliber. *Manias, Panics and Crashes: A History of Financial Crises.* Palgrave, Basingstoke and New York, 2005.

Kynaston, David. *The City of London: A Club No More, 1945–2000.* Chatto and Windus, London, 2001.

Lewis, Michael. *Liar's Poker.* Norton, New York, 1989.

Lowenstein, Roger. *When Genius Failed: The Rise and Fall of Long-Term Capital Management.* London, 2000.

Morris, Charles R. *The Trillion Dollar Meltdown: Easy Money, High Rollers, and the Great Credit Crash.* Public Affairs, New York, 2008.

Partnoy, Frank. *F.I.A.S.C.O: Blood in the Water on Wall Street,* Norton, New York, 1997..

Paulos, John Allen. *Innumeracy: Mathematical Illiteracy and Its Consequences.* Penguin, London, 1990.

Posner, Richard A. *A Failure of Capitalism.* Harvard University Press, Cambridge, Mass,, 2009.

Smith, Adam. *The Money Game.* Vintage, New York, 1976.

Taleb, Nassim Nicholas. *Fooled by Randomness: The Hid-*

den Role of Chance in Life and the Markets. Penguin, London, 2004.

Tett, Gillian. *Fool's Gold: How the Bold Dream of a Small Tribe at J.P. Morgan Was Corrupted by Wall Street Greed and Unleashed a Catastrophe.* Free Press, New York, 2009.

I have also been helped by the work of a number of journalists and commentators. I'd say, as an outsider to economics, that the standard of reporting and writing and commentary in this milieu is bracingly high. I have learnt an enormous amount from the work of Evan Davis, Stephanie Flanders, and Robert Peston at the BBC—Flanders and Peston have high-quality blogs, in addition to their old-media work; Philip Coggan, John Kay, Gillian Tett, and Martin Wolf at the *Financial Times;* Larry Elliott at *The Guardian;* and although as a Nobel Prize winner he is too grand to count, Paul Krugman at *The New York Times* is also a superb journalist and commentator.

There is a great deal of lively economic commentary on the Internet, and the best clearinghouse for the debates is the superb blog run by Tyler Cowen and Alex Tabarrok, Marginal Revolution, at www.marginalrevolution.com.

NOTES

Full references for books can be found in the Sources.

INTRODUCTION

1 You can follow the progress toward the goals at http://
ddp-ext.worldbank.org/ext/GMIS/home.do?siteId=2.
The news is less bad than one might expect, providing
that you can swallow the fact that nothing is improving
in sub-Saharan Africa.

CHAPTER ONE: THE ATM MOMENT

1 John Allen Paulos, *Innumeracy: Mathematical Illiteracy
and Its Consequences,* p. x.
2 Ben Funnel, "Debt is capitalism's dirty little secret," *Financial Times,* June 30, 2009, quoting research by Société Général.
3 See www.economics.harvard.edu/pub/hier/2005/HIER
2068.pdf.
4 Paul Krugman, "All the President's Zombies," *The New
York Times,* August 23, 2009.

5 Simon Johnson, "The Quiet Coup," www.theatlantic
.com/doc/200905/imf-advice.

6 David Kynaston, *The City of London*. Volume IV: *A Club No More 1945–2000*, London, 2001, Chatto and Windus, p. 791

7 For the gory details, see John Kay at www.johnkay.com/politics/614.

8 From a research paper by Daniel Gros and Stefano Micossi at www.voxeu.org, an outstanding resource for economic research and debate: www.voxeu.org/index.php?q=node/1669.

9 Quoted by Robert Peston on his blog at www.bbc.co.uk/blogs/thereporters/robertpeston/2009/07/why_bankers_arent_worth_it.html.

10 Charles R. Morris, *The Trillion Dollar Meltdown: Easy Money, High Rollers, and the Great Credit Crash*, Public Affairs, New York, 2008, p. xii.

11 www.ft.com/cms/s/2/6ac06592–6ce0–11de-af56–00144 feabdc0.html.

CHAPTER TWO: ROCKET SCIENCE

1 The best version of this story is told in Peter Bernstein, *Against the Gods: The Remarkable Story of Risk*.

2 Warren Buffett, letter to shareholders, Berkshire Hathaway Annual Report, 2002.

3 Ibid.

4 My account here and in the next chapter draws heavily on Gillian Tett's superb book *Fool's Gold: How the Bold Dream of a Small Tribe at J.P. Morgan Was Corrupted by Wall Street Greed and Unleashed a Catastrophe*. It needs a little basic financial knowledge to follow her account, but if you have that, *Fool's Gold* reads like

a thriller—written by someone who was not just following the story but predicted its outcome.

5 Testimony to the Senate Committee on Agriculture, Nutrition and Forestry, 30 July 1998.

CHAPTER THREE: BOOM AND BUST

1 I'm indebted to a piece by Steven Malanga in *City Journal*: www.city-journal.org/2009/19_2_homeownership .html.

2 There is an excellent discussion of Enron and the impact of frauds in George Akerlof and Robert Shiller's book *Animal Spirits: How Human Psychology Drives the Economy, and Why It Matters for Global Capitalism.*

CHAPTER FOUR: ENTER THE GENIUSES

1 Again, I'm deeply indebted to Gillian Tett's account of the CDO industry.

2 Richard A. Posner, *A Failure of Capitalism*. I don't agree with all of Posner's analysis, but it is superbly clear and his book is well worth reading as an account of the financial crisis being based on what one might call rational mistakes.

3 Tett, *Fool's Gold,* p. 182.

4 Richard Bitner, *Confessions of a Subprime Lender: An Insider's Tale of Greed, Fraud, and Ignorance,* has been a great help to me in understanding the bad lending which underlay the crisis.

5 "Bank Accused of Pushing Mortgage Deals on Blacks," *The New York Times,* June 6, 2009.

6 "US Seeks Culprits for Subprime," *Financial Times,* August 8, 2007.

CHAPTER FIVE: THE MISTAKE

1 Text © The Nobel Foundation 2002.

2 This example is from the best account of the subject, Naseem Taleb's *Fooled by Randomness: The Hidden Role of Chance in Life and the Markets*. I have drawn on Taleb's ideas in this chapter.

3 From "The Objectivist Ethics" in Rand's *The Virtue of Selfishness*.

4 Greenspan's testimony can be read in full at http://over sight.house.gov/documents/20081023100438.pdf.

5 Again, I'm indebted to Bernstein, *Against the Gods*.

6 The speech can be read at www.terry.uga.edu/sanford/ speeches/life_value.html.

7 This and the following exchange with Philippe Jorion are taken from www.derivativesstrategy.com/magazine/ archive/1997/1296qa.asp. And www.derivativesstrategy .com/magazine/archive/1997/0497fea2.asp

8 I am indebted to Felix Salmon's superb article "Recipe for Disaster: The Formula That Killed Wall Street," *Wired,* February 23, 2009.

9 See Kevin Dowd, John Cotter, Chris Humphrey, and Margaret Woods, "How Unlucky Is 25-sigma?" at www .ucd.ie/bankingfinance/docs/wp/WP-08–04.pdf.

10 From Greenspan's testimony to the House Committee on Oversight and Reform, op. cit.

11 See www.ggmwealthadvisors.com/files/2007%20Fall% 20Newsletter.pdf.

CHAPTER SIX: FUNNY SMELLS

1 From Bernstein, *Against the Gods,* p. 290.

2 I'm indebted to Charles R. Morris, *The Trillion Dollar Meltdown: Easy Money, High Rollers, and the Great Credit Crash.*

3 There's a chilling account of it in his book *The Ascent of Money,* chap. 6.

4 www.fsa.gov.uk/pubs/other/turner_review.pdf.

5 Posner, A Failure of Capitalism, xii.

6 Quoted by Gillian Tett in *Fool's Gold,* p. 97.

7 Simon Johnson, "The Quiet Coup," op cit.

8 Paul Krugman, "Out of the Shadows," *The New York Times,* June 18, 2009

9 *Financial Times,* June 12, 2009

10 You can, amazingly, listen to this meeting in its entirety at *The New York Times*'s website.

11 "The Reckoning," *The New York Times,* October 3, 2008.

12 Michael Lewis and David Einhorn, "The End of the Financial World as We Know It," *The New York Times,* January 4, 2009.

13 Testimony to the House financial services committee. 4 February 2009.

14 Richard Posner, *A Failure of Capitalism,* p. 268.

15 "AIG Trail Leads to London Casino," *The Daily Telegraph,* October 18, 2008.

16 Quoted by Richard Bitner in *Confessions of a Subprime Lender: An Insider's Tale of Greed, Fraud, and Ignorance,* p. 117.

17 Ibid., p. 112.

18 Charles R. Morris, *Trillion Dollar Meltdown,* p. 77.

CHAPTER SEVEN: THE BILL

1 John Maynard Keynes, "Economic Possibilities for Our Grandchildren." From Essays in Persuasion. Volume IX of the Collected Writings of John Maynard Keynes, pp. 324 et seq.
2 Meena Thiruvengadam, U.S. Bailouts So Far Total $2.98 Trillion, Official Says *The Wall Street Journal,* March 31, 2009.
3 www.ritholtz.com/blog/2008/11/big-bailouts-bigger-bucks.
4 Interview with Bloomberg Television, 20 January 2009.

INDEX

accounting, 26, 28, 106, 231
Against the Gods (Bernstein), 149
AIG:
  bailout of, 39, 76–78
  in CDS market, 75–78, 201
aircraft industry, 227
Alternative Mortgage Transaction
  Parity Act (AMPTA), 100
Animal Spirits (Akerlof and
  Shiller), 145*n*
Annie Hall, 1–2
Apple, 34
appraisals, 128
arbitrage, 54–55
arms manufacturing, 200
Arthur Andersen, 106
Asano, Yukio, 18
asset price bubble, 176–77
assets, 10, 25–42, 106, 176
  in balance sheets, 25–34, 37–38,
    70, 120
  banks and, 25, 32–42, 70, 74,
    120, 194
  of businesses, 29–30, 34
  derivatives and, 38, 48–50, 52,
    57–58, 120, 205–6

  housing and, 96, 126, 130,
    176–77
  intangible, 30
  leverage and, 35–36, 41
  liquidity and, 28–29
  risk and, 37, 146, 165
  toxic, 37–38, 42, 75, 165,
    189
ATMs, 7–9, 176
Austen Riggs Center, 140–41
automobiles, automobile industry,
    1–2, 24, 40, 134, 197, 222
  in balance sheets, 27–28
  stocks in, 148–49

balance sheets, 25–35
  banks and, 25–34, 37–39,
    41–42, 70, 120, 205–7
  of businesses, 29–34, 37, 106
  of individuals, 27–29, 35
Baltimore, Md., 83–86, 127, 129,
    163
Bankers Trust, 150
banking, bankers, banks, 19–22,
    24–43, 169, 171–78, 216–20,
    222–30

245

Securities and Exchange
   Commission (SEC), 195
   credit ratings and, 209–10
   regulation and, 153, 186,
      189–92
securitization, 20, 22, 200
   derivatives and, 69–70, 74,
      113–14, 117–19, 122, 212
   risk and, 69–70, 125, 163, 165,
      212, 224
selling, sales, 34, 42, 104, 174, 203
   of bonds, 59, 61–63, 144
   derivatives and, 46–50, 52, 56,
      65, 67–68, 73–74, 120
   of equity, 58–59
   of houses, 28–29, 71, 89–90
   risk and, 151–52, 165, 224
Shiller, Robert, 106, 145*n*, 194
Simon, David, 83–84
Singapore exchange, 54
Skilling, Jeffrey, 106
small numbers, law of, 137
Société Générale, 51, 77
solvency, insolvency, 28–29
   of banks, 36–38, 40–43, 64,
      74–75, 120
Spain, 15, 40, 177, 214
   contracting economy of, 222–23
   housing in, 92, 110
special purpose vehicles (SPVs), 70,
      120
stairs, deaths caused by, 134–35
Standard & Poor's (S&P), 62, 114,
      151, 209
statistics, 160–62
Stefánsdóttir, Rakel, 9–10, 12
stock market, stocks, 22, 54–55,
      61, 76, 80, 101–11, 115, 226
   bubbles and implosions in, 3, 42,
      103–9, 142, 175–76
   derivatives and, 50–52, 54
   investing in, 59, 73, 101–7, 111,
      146–52, 158, 175, 192
   new-economy, 103
   1929 crash of, 152, 199, 213

October 1987 crash of, 142,
      151–52, 161–62, 164–65
   prices of, 102, 105–6, 109–10,
      147–51, 158, 174
structured investment vehicles
   (SIVs), 120
Summa de Arithmetica (Pacioli),
      26
Summers, Lawrence, 43, 74, 188

Taleb, Nassim, 53, 155–56
Tax Reform Act of 1986 (TRA),
      100
technology, 42, 104, 149, 155,
      166
terrorism, 2, 12, 18, 107
Tett, Gillian, 121, 193
Thatcher, Margaret, 199, 217, 222
   free-market capitalism and, 14,
      21, 24
   on housing, 87, 91, 98
   regulation and, 21, 195–96
torture, end of ban on, 18
tranching, 117–18, 122
Treasury, British, 181–82
Treasury, U.S., 43, 54, 64, 74,
      76–78
   AIG bailout and, 76, 78
   regulation and, 188–90
Treasury bills (T-bills), 29–30, 62,
      103, 118, 144, 208
   China's investment in, 109,
      176–77
Trichet, Jean-Claude, 92
Trillion Dollar Meltdown, The
      (Morris), 42
Troubled Assets Relief Program
      (TARP), 37, 189
Turner, Adair, 181
Tversky, Amos, 136–38, 141

UBS, 36, 120
uncertainty, 96
   fair value theory and, 147–48
   risk and, 55–56, 153, 163

John Lanchester is the author of three novels, *The Debt to Pleasure* (winner of the Whitbread first novel prize and Hawthornden Award), *Mr. Phillips*, and *Fragrant Harbour*, and a memoir, *Family Romance*. He is a contributing editor at the *London Review of Books*; his work has appeared in *The New Yorker*, *The New York Times*, *Granta*, *Esquire*, *The Observer*, and *The Daily Telegraph*. Lanchester was awarded the 2008 E. M. Forster Award by the American Academy of Arts and Letters. He lives in London.